PAY CHEQUES AND PLAY CHEQUES

PAY CHEQUES AND PLAY CHEQUES

RETIREMENT INCOME SOLUTIONS FOR CANADIANS

TOM HEGNA

STEVE TATE

ROBERT GAWTHROP

Table of Contents

Foreword

We face some daunting challenges in Canada, ranging from a fiscally stretched federal healthcare delivery system to disappearing private pensions. In addition, we have an unprecedented demographic "tsunami" that threatens to bankrupt high public sector pension liabilities and the social welfare system we so dearly cherish. Together, these forces could crush the retirement dreams of many hard-working Canadians, making the idea of a secure retirement impossible.

Fortunately, there are financial products and strategies that provide a beacon of hope in the midst of this gathering storm. It is possible to take control of your retirement and obtain guaranteed income for life without having to depend on the government or your former employer. Just because the government is being forced to cut back does not mean you should.

The question then becomes: "Are you prepared?" Regrettably, the answer for most is "No." Canadians are stuck in the mutual fund or GIC mindset and unaware of available strategies such as annuities, life insurance, and similar investment vehicles.

Enter Tom Hegna. Few individuals have made a multi-billion dollar impact on an industry. The authors and I share the common goal of helping people achieve a secure retirement using low-risk, actuarially sound financial products. For example, only annuities offer mortality credits, which reward you for living longer. Your mutual fund advisor, your stockbroker, or your retail bank can't do that. And that's not idle speculation; annuities and similar proven strategies are based on mathematical, scientific, and economic facts.

Following the groundbreaking success of his book *Paychecks and Playchecks: Retirement Solutions for Life* in the United States, Tom offers his "Canadianized" strategies, with the help of his co-authors, Steve Tate and Rob Gawthrop. I endorse the "science and math" wholeheartedly, and cannot imagine a Canadian family who could overlook the powerful financial strategies in this essential roadmap to a successful, worry-free retirement.

I've spoken and coached in 50 countries over the last 25 years, and I can assure you from personal experience that NO ONE is more qualified to share the "science and math" of secure retirement planning than Tom. His co-authors were the last piece of the puzzle. Steve and Rob were brilliant in taking these concepts and applying them to Canadian regulatory practices.

If you are looking to soar beyond today's usual financial advice - cancel the rest of your day and read this book. If you are exhausted from the wild volatility of the last decade's market turmoil - read this book. If you dream of spending the golden years of retirement focused on your grandkids instead of nervously checking your bank balance - read this book.

Anthony Morris
April 2014
International Speaker and Advisor Coach
www.anthonymorris.ca

Preface to the
Canadian Edition

We read Tom's book, *Paychecks and Playchecks: Retirement Solutions For Life*, when it came out and felt the need to first correct Tom's spelling of the word "cheque", then adapt and adopt Tom's important information for Canadians. We both agreed with the book's overall message that, in the past, someone used to take care of you and provide you with income in retirement, whether it was the government or your employer. Recently, however, the onus has been placed on the individual to provide for themselves in retirement. They have had limited-to-no warning that this transition would be happening and limited-to-no information provided to them to ensure that their savings will be sufficient to last their lifetime.

We set out to "Canadianize" Tom's book because we felt that, although the message was great, its full impact and relevance was not being realized. Due to the different economics, government programs, and savings options available, we wanted to ensure that Canadians had the ability to take responsibility for their own retirement and be able to provide themselves with guaranteed income for the rest of their lives.

In recent years, it seems as though the media have focused almost exclusively on the world's hardships—recessions, financial collapse, war, civil unrest, and so on. The truth is, we have faced such tumultuous times for centuries. Read the history books as far back as you please; they will all document the consistency of world change and troubled times. For us, it just feels different this time. The range of possible outcomes for our economy, our way of life, and our country as a whole is the widest that any of us can remember during our lifetime. In the current financial environment, with all of the government intervention and printing of money, we do not even know what is real or what information we can depend on. We could soon see deflation, or we could just as easily see hyperinflation. The economy could continue its pattern of slow recovery, but it could also very well plummet into the next Great Depression. These are truly not normal times.

One drastic consequence of the financial downturn and current go-nowhere economy is that traditional safety nets such as pensions are rapidly disappearing and social program benefits like the Canada Pension Plan (CPP) and Old Age Security (OAS) are being modified. This situation, of course, happens to coincide with the retirement of over 10 million Baby Boomers who crave the same lifetime benefits their parents had. The first group of Boomers turned 65 in 2012. Tom and Rob are both Baby Boomers too, while Steve's parents are amongst the first wave of Boomers. We all felt compelled to write this book as a necessary roadmap for those who want to retire successfully and comfortably. This book is not based on our opinions. It is the product of careful research. Tom has been speaking around the world on the topic of retirement planning for over a decade, Rob has been working with select clients for over 25 years, and Steve has been focusing on estate planning and investment strategies since 2006. This book will share with you the best strategies we have been able to discover for planning your golden years.

We are all fascinated by how excited people get when they find that a successful retirement is possible. They can have a retirement that is not only successful, but also worry-free; a retirement with the financial flexibility to handle unforeseen events and face unexpected economic times triggered by inflation, deflation, stock market, and real estate booms and busts. Regardless of the economy's present or future state, those who read this book will learn to retire with minimal risk and maximum satisfaction. Some people think this scenario is too good to be true. Others are skeptical. Here is what we say: The research is clear. There is one optimal way to retire. This book will lay out the math and science behind having a successful and stress-free retirement.

The front page article of the April 4, 2011 *Wall Street Journal* was the tipping point for Tom to begin writing this book in the US. The headline read, "Fed's Low Interest Rates Crack Retiree's Nest Eggs". The article focused on a gentleman by the name of Forrest

Yeager, a 91-year-old resident of Port Charlotte, Florida. With his Certificates of Deposit (American version of a Guaranteed Investment Certificate [GIC]) paying less than 1%, his remaining $45,000 of retirement savings was providing just a few hundred dollars per year—forcing him to withdraw principal to live his current lifestyle. He believes his money will run out before he dies. Other retirees mentioned in the article had moved their money to stocks or high-yield bonds, subjecting their only savings to significant risk while losing their peace of mind.

That was it for Tom. He realized he had to get the word out. You do not have to live like that! You do not have to settle for 1% CDs—in fact, you absolutely should not. Mr. Yeager could walk into almost any reputable insurance company in America today and be guaranteed a payout of over 20% each year for the rest of his life! Think about that—in his case, $9,000 per year with zero market risk (we will explain this more indepth in later chapters). The same investment products are available here in Canada. That article went on to say, "The longer the central bank keeps interest rates low to stimulate the economy, the more money it pulls out of the pockets of millions of savers." These low interest rates are part of the central banks' plan to help recapitalize the banks.

Canadian retirees or investors who prefer stability over growth, who have done everything right, have worked hard, saved their money, and stayed out of debt are the ones being punished by low interest rates.

Luckily, you do not have to put all of your retirement savings into the stock market or junk bonds—and again, you shouldn't. That, of course, does not mean you should not invest at least some of your money in stocks, bonds, real estate, or commodities. You should. But what is the right mix? If you ask 50 different financial advisors, you will get 50 different "opinions". Unfortunately, these opinions will most likely be sub-optimal. Instead of offering you our opinion, we are going to lay out for you the math and science behind a very simple retirement solution. It is so simple, in fact, that you will probably ask yourself, "Why doesn't every financial advisor know this?"

So there you have it: We wrote this book to provide simple and effective financial strategies for upcoming retirees. After almost every seminar Tom has given over the last 15 years (and Tom has given somewhere near 3,000) someone would inevitably come up and say, "You should write a book. You make this sound so simple." Well, it is simple and we are big believers in simplicity.

Whenever we offer advice on financial matters, we try to explain concepts as simply as possible. It is not that clients don't have the capacity to understand complex ideas, but most people just do not want or need their finances to be complicated. Besides, people rarely lose money in a simple product like a GIC, fixed annuity, or money market fund. No, it is usually some complicated investment scheme that sounded great at the time but that the investor did not understand.

Our last bit of advice before we begin: always do your homework. In the financial world, it is called due diligence. Research your broker or financial advisor. Call their references. Search for indicators of professionalism, ethics, and excellence. One good indicator is longevity (the longer someone has been in the business, the less likely they are doing something wrong or illegal). A good motto is "Time is the friend of those who do business the right way, and it's the enemy of those who don't." Look for professional designations (the letters after their name)—again, no guarantee that the person is not a crook, but it establishes some level of training, ethics, and professionalism. Look at the company they have aligned themselves with. Is it a reputable company? Can you do research on their recommendations? Will they cite their references for their recommendations? We want you to do your due diligence on our recommendations as well. That way, you will be fully confident and committed to a successful retirement.

So for Mr. Yeager and the millions of retirees just like him, this book is for you.

Robert Gawthrop
Steve Tate
April, 2014

Chapter 1

What Happened to Happily Ever After?

As Bob Dylan once sang, the times they are a changin'. Believe it or not, there was a time in this country when you could retire gracefully and worry-free. Your employer held a little going-away party, presented you a shiny gold watch, and gave you a guaranteed paycheque for life in the form of a nice pension to keep you comfortable and allow you to live happily ever after—just like the fairy tales of old.

This, unfortunately, is no longer the case. It is more than likely that upon retiring, you will not receive a pension. Like dinosaurs, these plans have been going extinct ever since companies realized it was cheaper to match employee contributions to a Registered Retirement Savings Plan (RRSP). The extinction of pension plans has been hastened by a number of alarming defaults, highlighting the dangers and pitfalls of the pension system.

So what is left for you? Your RRSP? Unless you have been hiding under a rock for the past few years, you know what happened in 2008. The financial system crashed. Stock prices plummeted. You are probably left with two-thirds (or less!) of what you had hoped to save just five years ago. With inflation and a volatile market ahead, savings alone might not be enough to ensure you the retirement you deserve. Given that many of us will live about 25 years or more after retirement, there is a real possibility that you could deplete your savings—hardly our definition of "golden years".

And what about Old Age Security (OAS) and Canada Pension Plan (CPP)? The monthly cheques seniors depend on are about to get a whole lot less dependable. Considering the nation's government deficits and the current demand to keep taxes low, OAS & CPP may take different forms in the future. You should be able to count on these cheques, but will they be enough?

The balance of this chapter will examine today's problems with retirement—and find tomorrow's solutions using hard evidence. We do not like opinions; we like facts. Mathematic, scientific, and economic facts. We are going to lay the facts out in front of you and help you decide the best course of action.

Pension Problems

Company pensions used to form the third leg of the retirement planning stool along with OAS, CPP, and savings. Defined benefit pensions (DBP) are great—who wouldn't want guaranteed income for life? It is just that DB pensions do not really exist anymore for most retirees.

In your father's day, workers could count on receiving a lifelong cheque from their former employers. For most companies, this simply is not economically feasible anymore. Given that retirees are living longer and Canadian companies face stiff competition in the global economy, defined contribution plans (DCP) and Group RRSPs became a better deal as businesses sought to boost profits and limit liabilities. Today, only about 20% of our workforce can claim a DBP after retirement, and most of those jobs fall under the government sector. And if you have been paying attention to the news, even government pensions are diminishing as federal and provincial budgets have been strapped for revenue, leaving pensions with a potential shortfall. Based on evidence that is available from Statistics Canada, Public Accounts, and other sources, the unfunded shortfall for public pension plans across the country likely exceeds $300 billion.

Many companies are watching their pension costs go through the roof because they failed to set aside enough money to fund the benefits and retirees are living longer. The plans also promised payments that were just too high based on current life expectancy. Additionally, due to market volatility and poor stock market returns over the past decade, the investments backing the pensions have underperformed. It therefore comes as no surprise that big corporations such as Sears Canada and Telus have completely frozen their defined benefit pension plan and shifted to defined contribution plans. The trend in companies has been to start contributing to DCPs and group RRSPs instead of traditional pension plans, which shifts more of the risks to the individual worker.

When a pension plan goes belly up in the U.S., the company

transfers its pension problems onto the government, which runs a program called the Pension Benefit Guarantee Corporation (PBGC). Like most government institutions, the PBGC is in the red. In Canada, pension plan governance is a provincial responsibility so there is no federal government equivalent to the PBGC. The province of Ontario does have something called the Pension Benefits Guarantee Fund, but it only insures pensions up to $1000/month and only in the province of Ontario. Other provinces have regulations that require any pension shortfalls be made up by the sponsoring company within a certain period of time (usually between 5 and 10 years). But what happens if the sponsoring company goes bankrupt?

While we would like to say that only the most mismanaged companies default on pensions, sadly, that is not the case. It does not always occur because of incompetent management; market innovations and competition play a key role as well. Take Nortel, for instance. They were a huge enterprise with numerous product innovations through the years. Then, with increased competition in the fiber optics, internet, and general tech fields and the subsequent crash from the tech bubble in 1999 to 2000, Nortel became a casualty. Now Nortel is gone and their pension plan may not be far behind! Nortel pensioners have already seen their pension benefits be reduced by a minimum of 25%. Nortel pensioners have already seen their pension benefits be reduced by a minimum of 25%. Two decades ago, few would have predicted this dramatic turn of events. The point is, you probably do not have a pension, and you might need to worry about a default if you do. It is an unfortunate fact that this is the case, because there really is nothing like a guaranteed lifetime income stream. In this book we will help you to discover how to create your own guaranteed lifetime income.

The Panic of 2008 and What it Means for Your RRSP

You know what happened in 2008. If you have even glanced at a newspaper in the past six years, you know what happened. Globally, the statistics say it all: millions of lost jobs and trillions of government dollars went to troubled businesses, banks, and whoever else qualified for a handout. A 35% free fall in the S&P TSX. The last one hurt the most. Those who didn't know about the strategies we will share with you got hit pretty badly. A decade's worth of gains was wiped out. The era of steady double-digit returns was a distant memory.

Fast forward to 2014—the markets have recovered from the 2008 crash. But guess what? Many people were not in the market to see the recovery. If you think about it, these people lost TWICE—once when the market crashed and again when the market recovered its losses but they had sold at the bottom. This is still a whole new world for your retirement savings.

For one, individuals and institutions are not going to be as willing to invest their money in risky ventures like we saw in the subprime mess. On the bright side, we probably will not see another big stock market bubble or real estate bubble anytime soon, although there are some who predict Canada may still see a real estate bubble. But you have to remember that over the long term, those who understand risk, win. A market without much risk is a market without much opportunity.

There is another hidden aspect to this great recession. After we finally pull ourselves out of it, get back out there, and get paid, we may get hit with serious long-term inflation. The U.S.

government printed a lot of extra cash to avoid the worst of the recession. Once the downturn is over, what happens?

All those extra printed dollars are just going to be floating around, and it is going to cost more of them to get the same products. It is very easy for governments to print money, but it is much more difficult to pull it back out: doing so causes unemployment to rise and stocks to fall. For the long term, you have to keep inflation in mind.

These price-inflated products will include two resources retirees cannot go without: oil and food. Despite some fluctuation from shifts in both domestic and foreign markets, oil and food are steadily becoming more expensive. Crude oil prices, which hovered around $60 a barrel in 2006, shot up to over $100 a barrel by April 2011. This is inflation at its worst, nearly doubling the cost of oil in only five years. It permeates the economy from gas prices to the cost of shipping goods to market.

Food prices have also been rising over that same period. Just see what it costs today for a loaf of bread compared to five years ago. The consumer price index (CPI) measures the rate of price change of a basket of goods in Canada. Recent figures state our inflation rate is less than 2 % but over longer periods the rate has been much higher. Then there is the "stealth" food inflation—items ranging from canned tuna fish to potato chips are shrinking in portion size by 10-20%. The price may be the same, but you are getting less for your money.

Retirees are therefore facing a double whammy from low returns and higher prices. You cannot count on getting large returns for your money anymore. You probably can count on your diminished returns buying you less for your dollar.

The Old Age Security (OAS) & Canada Pension Plan (CPP) Dilemma

You have probably heard about some of the troubles with Old Age Security (OAS) and Canada Pension Plan (CPP). There are 10 million Baby Boomers in Canada (about 28% of the population), and every last one of them is rushing headlong into retirement. One by one, each Baby Boomer will soon stop working, stop contributing to CPP, and start taking money from the programs. Payroll taxes and individual contributions are used to fund the CPP program. With fewer workers contributing and an increase in those collecting CPP in retirement, this could cause significant pressure on the government's ability to meet the obligations. The OAS program is financed from Government of Canada's general tax revenue. In the 60s, the Feds reduced the age to qualify for OAS from 70 to 65 years old. Recently, we have seen them reversing this trend. For those born after January 1962, you will have to wait until age 67 before you are eligible to receive OAS.

Furthermore, the monthly benefit payments certainly will not be enough to cover average living expenses. Service Canada reported that the maximum monthly benefit for CPP at age 65 was $1012 in January 2013, however, the average monthly CPP benefit for senior citizens received was $534. Add the average current monthly OAS benefit at 65 of $515 and that still only amounts to just over $1000/month. But even assuming $1,000 monthly payments, $12,000 a year simply cannot cover all of a typical retiree's costs, and these circumstances are not going to improve.

For all of their problems, CPP and OAS were actually quite workable when they were first created back in the 1950s (OAS) and 1960s (CPP). The payments were sizable, and they kept a lot of older folks above the poverty line without breaking the government's credit. Here is the problem, though: during this era, there were far fewer beneficiaries compared with the number of workers paying into the system because people did not live as long as they do today. The average life expectancy in 1951, when the federal government first established the Old Age Security Act, was age 66 for men and age 71 for women. It was fairly typical for Canadians to pass away before they even reached age 65 and retired, leaving more OAS money to the lucky few blessed with longevity. The situation is much different today, with people often living into their 80s or 90s or even over 100!

Life Expectancy in Canada (1920 - 2010)

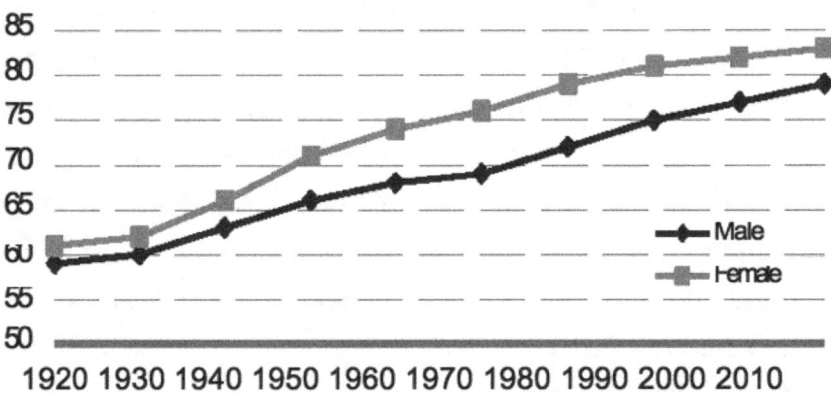

Source: World Bank, 2014

Recent data indicates the average lifespan for women has gone from 74 years in 1960 to roughly 83 today and from 68 to 79 years for men. This means that CPP and OAS will have to accommodate an unprecedented and overwhelming number of healthy, long-living retirees. Moreover, if you are married, you can count on an even longer average lifespan—by up to nine years.

So, what can you expect from CPP and OAS in the future? While cutting benefits or raising the age at which you could start collecting would have been political suicide just 10 years ago, the global financial crisis has permanently changed things. No one can predict where OAS benefits will be 10 years from now, but do not count on them being anywhere near as generous as they once were.

All this being said, we are not CPP & OAS doom-and-gloomers. We can confidently say that you will receive these pensions in retirement. The entire "problem" will not be that difficult to solve. It is a matter of understanding the economic realities and having the political will. In fact, one simple change would fix the system for the rest of our lifetimes; by gradually raising the retirement age by one month for every two years that you are younger than age 50. For instance, Rob's dad got full OAS at age 65, as will Rob; Rob's younger siblings won't get theirs until age 67. Is it that unreasonable that Rob's 16-year-old daughter won't get hers until 69 or 70? Her life expectancy will be longer than Rob and his father's, after all.

Overall, though, CPP & OAS will survive in some form. Future retirees might not get their parents' benefit amount in real (inflation-adjusted) terms, but they will receive these cheques in retirement and it will be greater in nominal dollars than what their parents received.

Canada Pension Plan (CPP) - By the Numbers

Contributors in 2013: 13.5 Million
Contrbutors by 2020: 14.5 Million
Contributions in 2013: $42 Billion
Contributions by 2020: $46 Billion
Retirees Collecting Benefits in 2013: 4.6 Million
Retirees Collecting Benefits by 2020: 6 Million
Retirees Collecting Benefits by 2050: 10.2 Million
Spending in 2013: $28 Billion
Spending by 2020: $43 Billion
Spending by 2050: $174 Billion

Source: Employment and Social Development Canada, 2014

The Rest of the World

It is a small comfort to know that we are not alone in facing large deficits and retirement anxieties. Japan's debt is larger than ours as a percentage of its Gross Domestic Product (GDP)— and that was before the earthquake and tsunami. You have probably heard about the political unrest in Greece and Ireland over budget austerity measures that became a necessity due to huge deficits. A driving force behind these budget shortfalls involves liabilities in government-funded retirement benefits.

The European Union is facing many of the same challenges in its retirement system that we are: Baby Boomer retirement, longer life spans, and reduced birthrates. According to *The Financial Times*, there are currently four workers per retiree. However, the ratio is expected to dwindle to two workers per retiree over the next 50 years. Fewer workers means less money will be available to pay for retirement benefits. The situation in Europe is exacerbated by the fact that workers there tend to retire earlier. In France, for example, the retirement age was 60. A proposal to raise it to 62 sent people into the streets! In Greece, it has not been uncommon for people in their late 40s and early 50s to retire with full pensions. Yet, scaling back benefits and raising the retirement age are the only real options. Reduced benefits, though, will mean a lower standard of living unless workers come up with new approaches for closing the "pension gap".

Europe may sound depressing, but what about China? The Chinese have experienced phenomenal economic growth over the past decade and they have enjoyed huge trade surpluses with the U.S. It seems like most consumer goods are made there these days! China also purchases U.S. bonds, which enables the U.S. to fund their big deficits. However, they, too, are in a race with the retirement tsunami. According to the Center for Strategic and International Studies, there were 16 retirees for every 100 workers in 2005, making China a relatively young country. This ratio is expected to double to 32 retirees by 2025, and double again to 61 retirees per 100 workers by 2050! That translates into 438 million Chinese over 60 years old by mid-century. By 2030, China will actually be an older country than the U.S. with respect to the ratio of workers to retirees. It has been said that while India will get rich before it gets old, China will get old before it gets rich. This age wave could create problems for their economy and will put pressure on the government to devise solutions.

The point is, we are not the only ones going through a rough patch, and other countries may have to deal with much worse.

Now is not the time to mope over what happened—instead, it is a time to look forward, look up, and find new answers to new problems.

Who Will Sign your retirement Paycheque?

This is not a book about how CPP and OAS will not give you a cheque when you retire, nor is this a book explaining why your company's CEO mismanaged your pension fund. It is not about the people who used to sign the cheques for retirement income. This is a book about who is going to sign that retirement income cheque in the future.

So if neither the government nor your former employer will be signing your retirement paycheque...who will? It just might be your insurance company. Annuities (financial contracts with an insurance company) can afford you a guaranteed income for life. In a world without stable pensions or reduced CPP and OAS benefits, annuities are quickly becoming a hot new item for retirement income.

The June 20, 2011 cover of *Barron's* magazine focused on annuities: "With investors clamoring for steady flows of income, it's time to give annuities a fresh look."

In 2009, the Federal Provincial Territorial Ministers of Finance released their report from the Research Working Group on Retirement Income Adequacy. The full report is available online. It says "about one in 10 Canadians will live 10 years past their normal life expectancy. The sharing of longevity risk through life annuities can theoretically enable individuals to earn significantly more income over time."

Now that we just spent a chapter going over every hardship, difficulty, and obstacle standing between you and retirement, it is time to go over some solutions. Like we said earlier, we do not care for opinions. We like facts. One fact you are going to like is that you can still have the retirement of your dreams. You can have a guaranteed stream of income for the rest of your life. You can have something to give your grandkids. It is a mathematic, scientific, and economic fact that you can cover expenses and still see your savings grow.

We firmly believe in the saying that life does not close a door without opening a window. You should not worry about a lost pension or a reduced or postponed CPP or OAS cheque—you should be thinking about how to expand your annuity IQ and develop an appropriate asset and product allocation system. There are plenty of ways to make your retirement happy and prosperous.

It is a brave new world out there, and we are here to help you find your retirement solution.

What Happened to Happily Ever After?

 Key Points from Chapter 1

1. Traditional safety nets of retirement income are changing. Pensions, CPP and OAS will not provide the level of income your parents received.

2. The economic collapse of 2008 has shaken people's confidence. The volatility of the markets, the printing of trillions of dollars, and civil unrest around the world due to government austerity measures have all caused people to doubt the viability of their retirement.

3. These issues are affecting retirees around the world, not just in Canada.

4. Who is going to sign YOUR monthly retirement cheque?

5. This book will help answer that question.

Chapter 2

The Distribution Dilemma: Just the Facts

Saving for retirement, especially in the current economic climate, can be challenging enough. However, how you draw down and distribute your retirement savings once the bell sounds and your career is over, will determine whether or not you run out of money. This distribution dilemma and the various risks to your nest egg once you retire are the focus of this chapter.

Saving for Retirement: The Easy Part?

We are constantly bombarded with ads for various retirement savings plans from brokers, mutual fund companies, and financial planning firms, just to name a few. Most of these planning options focus on the accumulation phase: the time while you are working and saving for retirement. They provide you with a plethora of investment options, as well as hypothetical growth rates on your principal. They will make an estimate of how much you will need to accumulate by the time you retire. You deposit a little each month into your RRSP or Tax-Free Savings Account (TFSA), or both, and gradually build up your savings to your supposed "magic number".

Accumulating money is an important first step on the road to retirement. Our advice is to start early and to not make assumptions that are too rosy. The sooner you can start putting money in a retirement savings account like an RRSP or TFSA, the better. In 2010, the average Canadian household saved only 4.5% of their disposable income. While most people who are actively saving for retirement think that saving 10% is enough, we recommend that no less than 15% of your income should be directed to long-term savings. As you approach retirement, try to make it 25%. "Wait 'til next year" might be a great sports cliché, but it is not a good plan for retirement savings. The longer you wait, the more you will have to play catch up, which means you will have to dedicate larger amounts each year to your retirement accounts and take on significantly more risk in order to achieve your goals. A quote from Noel Whittaker, which seems appropriate here, is "Life is full of uncertainty. Future investment earnings and interest and inflation rates are not known to anybody. However, I can guarantee you one thing: those who put an investment program in place will have a lot more money when they come to retire than those who never get around to it." Again, you should guard against rosy scenarios. There is research that suggests that salaries tend to plateau by your early to mid-40s. From that point on, it is likely that you will not receive much beyond a cost-of-living adjustment. Also, if you lose a job in your

50s, it can be difficult to find another one at an equivalent salary. Given these facts, you need to save for retirement early, since you cannot count on big salary increases later in your career.

As you approach retirement, you may notice that you fixate more and more on wealth accumulation. However, accumulation is actually only a small part of the equation at this stage. Assuming you have a steady job or some other stream of income during your pre-retirement years, adding money to savings should technically be the easiest part of retirement planning. If the market dips, you can make up for the losses in your investments by contributing more to your retirement savings, which you are not spending at the moment anyway. However, the day you retire, the rules change! Now you are spending assets instead of accumulating them. Even if you save up to your goal of $1 million or $5 million or whatever amount you decide, you could still squander it all away in poor investments or by withdrawing it too quickly. In truth, there is no magic retirement number. The accumulation phase is only the end of the beginning, whereas the distributions from your savings must last until the end.

Distributing assets in a way that ensures you get the most out of your retirement without running out of money is a difficult balancing act, and should be taken even more seriously than your accumulation phase. Some retirees never do anything for enjoyment in retirement. Why not? They are so afraid of losing money that they invest in ultra-low-yielding investments—like low-interest GICs, or, as we say, "Guaranteed Depreciation Certificates". Others may invest more wisely, but will not spend a nickel for the same fear of running out of funds. Still, others spend wildly in the early years of their retirement only to find out that their spending, and the never-ending curse of inflation, has now relegated them to near-poverty for the rest of their years. So, when planning your golden years, think less about how much you have and more about how you will spread out what you have so that it will last the rest of your life. The next section will examine the risks you need to consider when figuring out the right accumulation and distribution strategies for your retirement.

Retirement Risks

LONGEVITY RISK

People are living longer than ever before. The average 65-year-old male will live to age 85, while the average 65-year-old female will live to 88. But what's the problem with averages? The problem is that they have nothing to do with how long any one individual will live. Half of everyone reading this book will live longer than their gender's average life expectancy, while half will not. Life expectancy is not an average at all; it is simply a mid-point. Half of all 65-year-old men will die prior to age 85, but the whole other half will remain alive. Half of all 65-year-old females will die prior to age 88. The other half? All alive. So averages are not at all an indicator of how long your retirement days will last—you need to operate under the notion that you very well may live long past your gender's average age of death.

Additionally, married people live longer than single people. We have no idea why, but it's a fact. If you have a husband and wife who are 65, there is a 50/50 chance that one of them will live to age 92. Think about that—think about all the 65-year-old couples you know. Fifty percent of them will have at least one member live to 92. There is a 25% chance one of them will live to 97. So if you are married, you really need to consider joint life expectancy. And there will be plenty of people reading this book who will live beyond age 100, especially considering medical innovations and rising life expectancy rates.

When planning for retirement income, you cannot plan to have income until age 90—you really need to plan to have income until age 100 and possibly beyond. That may seem like playing it a bit too safe, but it is not at all unreasonable if half of retirees are already living into their 90s. Depending on when you retire, your retirement savings will probably need to last for at least 25 years if not more. In addition, the longer you live, the more inflation can eat away at your savings if you are not careful. You will need an investment and withdrawal strategy that will last as long as you do.

LONGEVITY IS A "RISK MULTIPLIER"

It is also important to understand that longevity is not just a risk. It is a multiplier of the other risks. Because of this, our belief is that it is imperative that you transfer that risk to an insurance company. Because insurance companies utilize risk pooling, they are perfectly positioned to manage longevity risk. The risk when companies sell life insurance is that someone dies too soon; the risk when they sell a Lifetime Income Annuity is that someone lives too long. Because they are on both sides of the risk, they perfectly hedge longevity risk. No other industry can do this. Let us explain why removing longevity risk is so important to the success of your retirement.

If you retire at age 65 and die at age 68, it would not matter if the stock market dropped 40%. It would not have mattered if you had withdrawn 12% per year, or if inflation increased by double digits, or if you did not buy a long-term care policy. You did not live long enough for any of that to matter. However, if you lived to age 100, any one of those things would have devastated your retirement. The risks of needing long-term care skyrocket with longevity. So if you ask us what the biggest risk in retirement is, we would say hands down it is longevity risk, simply because it has a multiplier effect on all of the other risks.

WITHDRAWAL RATE RISK

Another fact we have observed: people know how much money they have. Given the volatility in the financial markets in recent years, we have updated this observation a bit: now we say people know how much money they had. But in all seriousness, we do believe people still know how much money they have. With online banking and other financial services that have sprung up over the past few decades, it has become increasingly easy for upcoming retirees to keep full track of their finances. The real problem is that once people have a good idea of how much they have saved, they are not quite sure what to expect from it or how to use it. Distribution strategies play a key role here, so it is paramount that you take into account withdrawal rate risk.

The amount you distribute or withdraw from your retirement savings, when examined in conjunction with your lifespan, will determine whether you live comfortably or run out of money. Let us look at a simple example without factoring in inflation or investment performance. Suppose you retired at 65 with $100,000 in retirement savings and started withdrawing about $5,000 per year (5%). If you lived for 10 more years, you would still have $50,000 left to pass on to your loved ones. However, if you lived 30 more years to age 95, and withdrew that same amount ($5,000 per year), you would be out of money by age 85! The next 10 years would be tough since your retirement savings would be exhausted. The bottom line is, the longer you live, the greater the risk of depleting your savings unless you adjust your withdrawal rates downward.

A major American insurance company did a study about this in 2008. It said that 43% of all Baby Boomers believe they can take out 10% per year or more from their portfolio in retirement. Well, you can, but you're going to run out of money very quickly. *The Wall Street Journal* had an article that explained the bulletproof withdrawal rate for a diversified portfolio. What is your guess, 5%? Wrong—too much. Even a 4% withdrawal rate fails 20% to 30% of the time depending on what investment model and assumptions you use. So what is the bulletproof rate? Only 2%! *The Wall Street Journal* said that 2% is the bulletproof withdrawal rate, although 3% is considered safe. Alternatively, 4% is pushing it, and with 5% or more you will probably run out of money—it is only a matter of time. Most people have no idea how dangerous it is to withdraw too much each year. You see, after longevity risk, withdrawal rate risk is one of the biggest challenges you will face in retirement.

ORDER OF RETURN RISK

As you surely know, the market can take swift turns up and down. What matters to you, however, as a saver or investor, is the average return from your investments over a period of years. But the day you retire and start taking money out of a portfolio, all the rules change and average returns are no longer important. This statement probably goes against what most retirees think. It certainly goes against what you have experienced, because for your whole life, you have been a saver and an investor. You have grown used to checking the average returns on your RRSPs, your TFSAs, your stocks, bonds, and mutual funds. If you can get a 3% average return, it's better than 1%. And if you can get 5%, it's of course better than 3%. So we grow up thinking that average returns are what really matter.

You might be thinking like Jim. The year was 1973. He had $100,000. He invested 50% in stocks and 50% in bonds. Over the following 22 years, Jim averaged a 10.1% return per year! His money grew to approximately $846,000—and it does not matter if we run the numbers backwards from 1995 to 1973 because he still averaged 10.1% per year. Jim still wound up with a boatload of money, regardless of the sequence of his yearly returns.

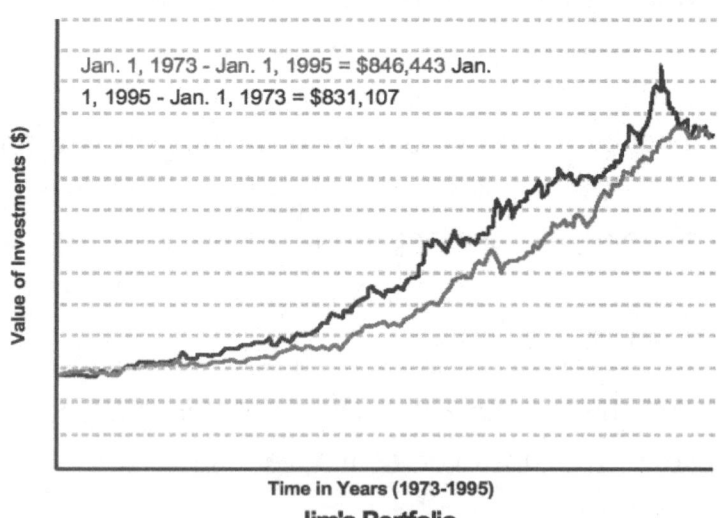

Jan. 1, 1973 - Jan. 1, 1995 = $846,443 Jan. 1, 1995 - Jan. 1, 1973 = $831,107

Time in Years (1973-1995)
Jim's Portfolio

Source: New York Life Investment Management LLC, 2004

That's the way some people think the world works, but it does not work that way the day you retire. Consider Bill, who also had $100,000 in 1973. Just like Jim, he invested 50% of it in stocks and the other half in bonds. He also averaged 10.1% a year for 22 years. However, Bill retired in 1973 and needed income, so his financial advisor told him he could take out 5% per year. With an average yearly return of twice that, both Bill and his advisor figured everything would be fine. The result? He is dead broke. Now you are wondering, how can you average 10.1% a year for 22 years, take out 5% a year, and go broke? The short answer is, average returns don't matter—the 10.1% yearly average has nothing to do with the sequence, or order, of returns over the years. The day you retire, there is only one thing that matters, and that is the order of those returns.

You may remember what happened to the stock market between 1973 and 1975: the market went down for three consecutive years. Here's the deal: if the market goes down for the first few years of your retirement (assuming your assets are in a diversified

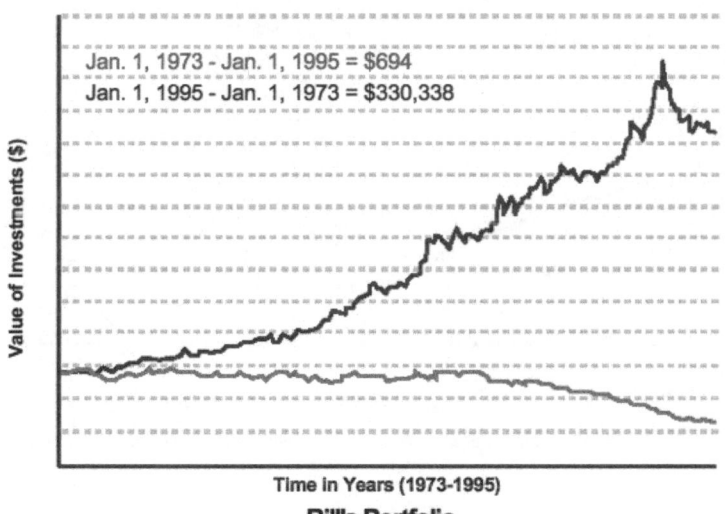

Jan. 1, 1973 - Jan. 1, 1995 = $694
Jan. 1, 1995 - Jan. 1, 1973 = $330,338

Value of Investments ($)

Time in Years (1973-1995)
Bill's Portfolio

Source: New York Life Investment Management LLC, 2004

portfolio), you are going to be in trouble. You will either have to put in more, take out less, or you will run out of money. The order of returns is crucial in this scenario; losses in the first few years of retirement can devastate your portfolio.

Take a look at the chart below; this is also going to oppose everything you have been taught. We think almost all financial advisors were taught that the older you are, the more con-servatively you should invest. For example, that an 80-year-old should invest more conservatively than a 60-year-old and that the 60-year-old should invest more conservatively than a 40-year-old. However, that is not what this chart shows. Both of these portfolios have identical "average returns". What is the dif-ference between the two portfolios? The dark line shows the portfolio that lost money early in retirement, and you can see that it devastated these people's retirement. The lighter line shows a portfolio that lost money later in retirement, and it had much less of an impact on the person's retirement.

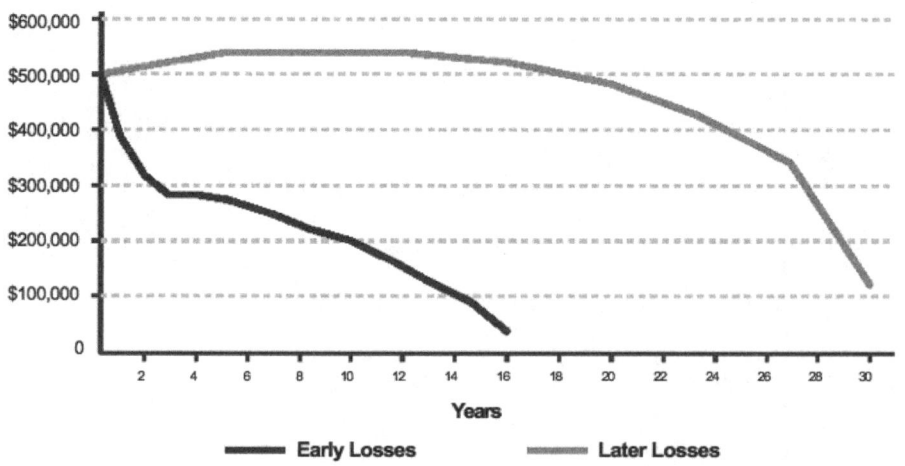

Source: New York Life Investment Management LLC, 2004

A study done June 2011 discussed the order of returns risk and provided the following example based on a $100,000 initial investment at age 65 and assumes a 9% annual withdrawal rate. It also projected that the returns below would repeat every three years. The chart on the next page shows how long an investment with a 7% average annual return could last, depending on the order of the returns. The report noted "if the sequence of returns in the second and third year were reversed, holding all else constant, the average annual return would be the same; yet, if withdrawals are made each year, savings would be depleted sooner with the first sequence of returns." This example illustrates the danger of depending on a volatile stock market when you need retirement income. Even an up market may not provide the security you need once you retire and start taking out money.

Year 1	Year 2	Year 3	Average Return	Years Until Depleted
+7%	-13%	+27%	+7%	18
+7%	+27%	-13%	+7%	24

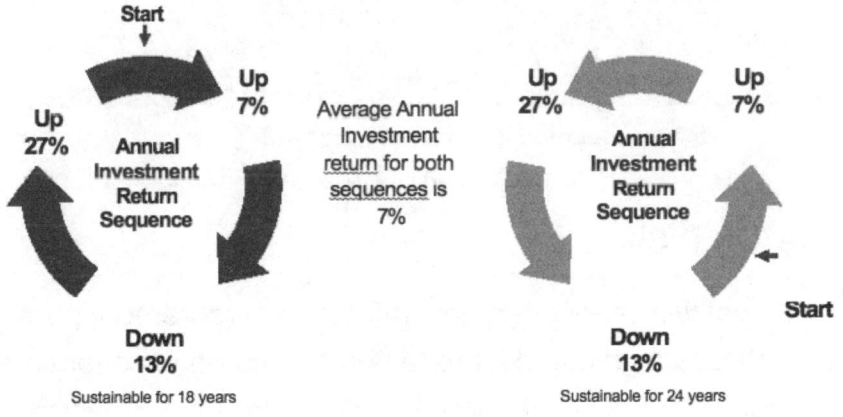

Source: GAO Report - Retirement Income, June 2011, p. 16

The order of returns risk is greatest in the years right before and right after you retire. Big market declines, like we saw in 2008 to 2009, that occur during this time frame, could be devastating to your retirement savings and future income. Many advisors believe that the older you are, the more conservative your investments should be. But in reality, the years right before and after the beginning of your retirement matter far more than those later years. So if you asked us, "When is the riskiest, most critical time for a retiree, when they really should not mess anything up?" It is right here. If you want to pick a time in your life to not lose money, that period would be the last five or six years that you are working and the first five or six years of retirement. Prudential made this concept famous with their "Retirement Red Zone", and they were absolutely right.

Market risk is greatest in years just before and after retirement

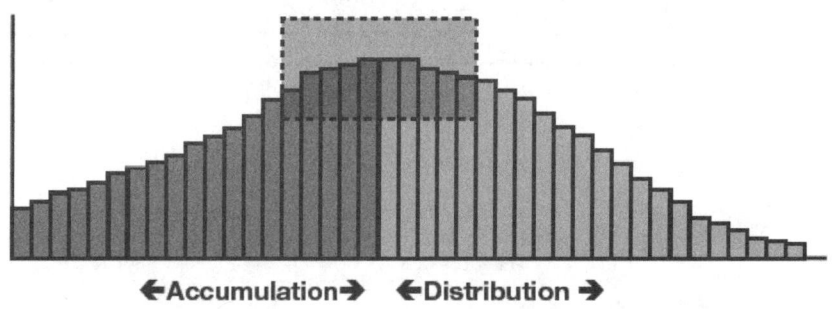

←Accumulation→   ←Distribution →

Source: New York Life Investment Management LLC, 2004

INFLATION RISK

One risk that will almost certainly affect every retirement portfolio is inflation, which can decimate purchasing power over time. For example, if you get $3,000 per month from your nest egg, the purchasing power at 4% inflation will be cut by more than half in 20 years and by more than two-thirds in 30 years. Even if inflation averages only 3% per year over the next 15 years, you will need about $4,700 per month to match the purchasing power of $3,000 in today's dollars. There have been some periods, such as the late 1970s, when inflation soared into the double digits.

Inflation is extremely problematic for retirees who are on fixed incomes and who are depending on their retirement savings to help make ends meet. High inflation can erode both your income and your portfolio if you do not plan for it. Canada has experienced a period of relative price stability and low inflation for the past 25 years. Even so, prices of food, gas, postage, and other items you buy have gone up significantly over this same period. Many Canadians are very worried about inflation right now, especially considering the recent activities of quite a few of the world's central banks, most notably Japan and the Federal Reserve in the U.S., who, as a result of the aftermath of the financial panic, have taken drastic measures to defeat an economic collapse.

While Canada was able to weather the financial storm a few years ago, or at least better than most countries, the U.S. was not so lucky. Canada lowered its interest rate slightly, but nowhere close to the near 0% of the U.S. What is going on in the U.S. right now will have an effect on the Canadian economy and already does. Along with holding interest rates extremely low, over the past few years, the Federal Reserve has printed nearly $3 trillion worth of money in the form of "Quantitative Easing 1", "Quantitative Easing 2", and "Quantitative Easing 3". We know not all of you are economics majors, but what happens to the value of a dollar every time you print another dollar? It goes down. Well, if the value of the dollar goes down, what happens when you go to buy something? You need more dollars. This is inflation. When the government prints money, it causes inflation—eventually and inevitably. But what many people do not realize is that printing money alone does not cause inflation. Janet Yellen, the Federal Reserve chairman as of this writing, could print $5 trillion, but if she had dug a hole and buried it, there would be no inflation. The money has to make its way into the economy to have any impact on inflation.

This second and equally important component of inflation is called the velocity of money. It is a measurement of how fast money turns over in the economy based on the amount of economic activity. If we assumed normal money velocity, the Fed's printing of nearly $3 trillion would have not only caused inflation, but hyperinflation. But these are not normal times, and economic activity has plunged due to the recession and ensuing rise in unemployment. Therefore, the money that the U.S. government has printed has not fully worked its way into the economy.

Some economists will say that the Fed's policy has worked its way into commodity markets, causing oil, gas, gold, silver, and agricultural product prices to soar. We will find out soon how all of that ends. The website SeekingAlpha.com recently had an article we found to be quite timely. It read, "What we are seeing right now is inflation in everything you OWE (like food, gas, and medicine) and deflation in everything you OWN (like real estate)." They went on to call it a "toxic combination".

It is extremely important for you to protect your retirement assets from inflation, since inflation increases the risk that you will run out of money. There are financial strategies to deal with inflation during retirement, such as purchasing inflation protection on a Lifetime Income Annuity. In addition, you can self-insure your portfolio against inflation by boosting your retirement savings while you are still working. Suppose your goal was to save $100,000 for retirement. You could get 25 years of inflation protection for your annual withdrawals if you started your retirement with $160,000, assuming a 3% inflation rate and 6% average return on your portfolio.

DEFLATION RISK

Deflation might be just as big a risk to retirees as inflation. Deflation is the reverse of inflation and means a decline in the overall price of goods and services. You may be wondering: why would declining prices be a bad thing? There are several reasons. First, deflation or falling prices would cause a dramatic slowdown in economic activity. Consumers and businesses would be reluctant to spend or borrow. Think about it: why buy something today if you could purchase the same item six months later for a lot less? You could just hoard your cash. Second, deflation would lead to a decline in wages and eventually trigger large job losses. In order to get workers to accept falling wages, companies would be forced to lay off large numbers of people. These factors, in turn, would drive us into a deep recession. Could we be in for a dangerous bout of deflation?

Deflation is triggered by a decline in the overall level of demand in the economy. Less demand translates to lower prices. As you have no doubt observed, falling prices are not a bad thing if they are due to mass production and/or cheaper overseas labor. Just visit a local Walmart. However, if price declines are caused by a lack of demand, the economy stagnates and contracts. We have already seen this happen in the United States real estate sector, and prices have tanked accordingly. However, there is another bubble ready to burst: we call it the government bubble. Governments around the world for the past 30 years have over-promised, and for the next 30 years they will be in the business of under-delivering. The deflationary impact of these changes in government policy could be devastating.

Recall that many foreign governments such as France, Ireland, and Greece have been cutting pensions and making changes to retirement plans. Sound familiar? The qualifying age for the OAS pension from the Canadian Government was recently pushed back from 65 to 67 years old. This means if you were born later than April 1st, 1958, you may have to wait up to 2 years longer to collect than someone born March, 31st, 1958. An analyst on the website SeekingAlpha.com actually recommended investing in tear gas. Can you believe that? As governments around the globe are forced to cut their programs, the number of riots and protests requiring police intervention and tear gas will spike. Beyond the political chaos, all of these government cuts will deflate the economy because there will be less money to spend.

Canada and its provinces are performing relatively well, compared to the rest of the world, when it comes to fiscal responsibility. While the long-term outlook for the CPP is actuarially sound, there are changes being made to ensure its ability to continue to provide Canadians with pension income in retirement. The burden of 10 million retiring Baby Boomers has already forced the

Government of Canada to make changes to the CPP and, in all likelihood, these changes won't be the last. Starting in 2012, and going until 2016, the early pension amount is gradually being decreased. If you retire early and start collecting your pension before the age of 65, you will receive less than what was previously being paid out. The CPP may be actuarially sound, but it is being changed and these changes are not to the benefit of those who are going to be receiving the pension. While these adjustments may cause some concern and may only be the tip of the iceberg so to speak, these problems are occurring all over the world. Some of the larger states in the U.S. (California, New York, New Jersey, and Illinois) are nearly bankrupt. In the summer of 2013, Detroit became the first major city in the U.S. to declare bankruptcy, and it is not expected to be the last. On the state and local level, the U.S. is facing about $3 trillion of unfunded government pensions. So there are going to have to be cuts upon cuts at the local level, as well as cuts upon cuts at the state level.

Canada, at the government level, is performing quite well, fiscally. However, Canadians as individuals are causing the federal government and the Bank of Canada some concern. Household debt, in comparison to income, is now at levels higher than the United States prior to 2008. Our property values never had the major correction that occurred in the U.S. and we need to hope that property values maintain their value in a cooling housing market. If we as Canadians cannot curb spending, if a major housing correction comes, it could have devastating results.

At the federal level, by the time you read this, our country will be over $600 billion in debt, with every person's individual share being over $17,000. The federal debt in the U.S. is far more worrisome than Canada's and, at the time of this writing, is over $17 trillion. With Social Security and Medicare, there are another $40 trillion of unfunded benefits to reckon with. Add Medicaid and now we are close to $123 trillion. Needless to say, an extraordinary number of cuts will be made on top of those that have already happened. These cuts in government spending are deflationary—less money in the economy means reduced demand and falling prices.

 One Trillion Dollars - By the Numbers

Most people don't really know what a trillion is besides the fact it rhymes with million and billion. Here is a very simple way to understand how much a trillion is: if one dollar equals one second, a million dollars would be about 11.5 days, and a billion dollars would be 32 years. A trillion dollars would be 32,000 years. Isn't that incredible—32,000 years...

There are also problems in the private sector that could cause deflation. We have already mentioned the real estate crash in the U.S. that caused the world's stock markets and economies to collapse. In addition, there are two other trends that point to decreased consumer demand and lower overall prices. Consider all of the mortgage debt, credit card debt, student loan debt, and corporate debt; all of this debt must be de-leveraged (paid down or reduced)! This de-leveraging is highly deflationary and economies around the world would be hit hard. Job creation and employment are only now starting to creep back to pre-recession levels, and all of this has been very deflationary, with growth only now showing the slightest hint of bringing change. The unemployment and underemployment numbers are some of the worst we have seen in the post-World War II era.

On top of all this, Baby Boomers are now officially over-the-hill when it comes to spending money. You will typically spend the most money between the ages of 45 and 50. This period is when you have two kids in university, two brand new cars, and the biggest home you have ever had. For years, Baby Boomers drove the economy as they wanted bigger and better and more of everything. Now, however, Boomers are well past their peak spending years, meaning they will spend less and less as they age. As we have noted, less spending means reduced demand, which is deflationary. Both Europe and Japan have demographic problems as well, and their people will be spending less and less each year for decades to come.

We never said, of course, that we could predict the future. But the bond market does, or at least tries, to do this every single day. You really have to watch the bond market. If you see interest rates rising, as we did unexpectedly in June of 2013, the smart money is seeing the possibility of future inflation. If you see interest rates falling, then expect possible deflation. What you are really looking for is one word: growth. If you see the economy picking up, unemployment falling, the housing market recovering, or the stock market rising, then the risk is inflation, since money velocity will pick up. Remember, homes are "real assets", which is why they are called "real estate". Real assets typically go up in times of inflation, not down. If you are looking for an inflection point where inflation and higher interest rates could happen, look for when unemployment numbers drop and housing prices bottom and start to move higher.

On the other hand, if you see a double-dip in housing, the stock market crashing, and unemployment rising, the risk is de-flation. It has become our mantra: these are not normal times. You have to be aware like never before. You cannot just "go with the flow." All of these economic headwinds are exactly why you need this book right now. So now that we have you good and depressed, are there any solutions? Yes, the rest of this book will focus on solutions.

The Distribution Dilemma:
Just the Facts

 Key Points from Chapter 2

1. Accumulating money may be the easiest part of retirement. Start early and save as much as you can—15% of your income would be a good start.

2. Understand that longevity is not just a risk in retirement; it is a RISK MULTIPLIER of the other risks.

3. The withdrawal rate risk is the risk of running out of money by taking too much out of your retirement savings each year. A 2% withdrawal rate is considered bulletproof, 3% is safe. Withdrawing 4% or more a year can cause your portfolio to run out of money.

4. Understand how the order of returns can have a dramatic impact on portfolio success.

5. The riskiest time to invest is right before or right after retirement. A loss during these years can have a devastating impact on your retirement savings.

6. Inflation is a risk that increases over time. With the amount of money being printed around the world and subsequently being injected into the economy, if we get any money velocity (increase in economic activity), we could see significant inflation.

7. Deflation may be the biggest risk in the short term. Governments around the world are cutting budgets and benefits to try to balance their books after borrowing unprecedented amounts to avoid an economic collapse a few years ago. Consumers from around the world are also reducing their debts. We, as Canadians, are being encouraged to cut our deficits and reduce our total debt levels, which are at an all-time high. Global demographics, especially for developed countries, will mean less spending and weaker economic growth, possibly for decades!

Chapter 3

Guaranteed Paycheques
and Playcheques

Income You Can Count On

The life insurance industry was built for markets like the ones we are facing now—life insurance and annuities can be the solution to many of today's personal finance dilemmas, as these products are based on math and science. There are a wide variety of annuities out there, and we will examine all of them in a later chapter. Right now, we are going to look closely at one: the lifetime income annuity. Many companies call it a SPIA—a Single Premium Immediate Annuity. It is an annuity that provides immediate, guaranteed income for life. We cannot stress enough how important this product is to a successful retirement. In fact, in order to retire in an optimal manner, you have to use this type of annuity.

For a moment, pretend we are your retirement planners so we can show you how simple this is. We are recommending that you purchase a lifetime income annuity so that you can have a great retirement. And the first thing you will probably ask us is, "Well, what is a lifetime income annuity?" Here are the words we use: it's a guaranteed paycheque for life. That's all it is: a guaranteed paycheque for life.

To make this even easier to understand, let us remind you that you already have a lifetime income annuity—your Old Age Security and Canada Pension Plan cheques. Remember, OAS & CPP are guaranteed paycheques for life. If you have a defined benefit pension, that is also a guaranteed paycheque for life. OAS, CPP, and DB pensions are examples of lifetime income annuities.

The Importance of the Playcheque

Now, every once in a while, we come across someone who says, "I don't need another guaranteed paycheque. I worked as a public school teacher for 37 years. I already have a pension—I've got that covered." Then we just smile and say, "Okay, you have the paycheque. But do you know what you need now? You need a guaranteed playcheque." See, we think seniors today need both a guaranteed paycheque and, perhaps just as importantly, a guaranteed "playcheque". Let us prove it to you.

On what day of the week do you spend the most money right now? What day of the week do you go golfing, go to Home Depot, go to the spa, or go shopping? For most of us, that day would be Saturday—and remember, when you retire, every single day is Saturday. Many Boomers are not going to need less money once they retire; they are going to need more money. So we would say that you do not need just a guaranteed paycheque, but a guaranteed playcheque as well. That's all a lifetime income annuity is.

Old Age Security/Canada Pension Plan & other Pensions—Weak Legs of the Stool

Historically, the ideal retirement consisted of three basically equal components—OAS/CPP, a company pension, and personal savings. This was illustrated graphically with the picture of a three-legged stool such as the one below. Today, however, there are problems with all three legs. Old Age Security is starting to be tinkered with. Some will not start to receive it now until age 67. While we have no doubt that you will receive OAS benefits in retirement, you will not necessarily get what your parents received, and you definitely will not see as much inflation protection as your parents saw. The company pension plan, as we discussed earlier, is becoming extinct for almost everyone other than government workers. Even government workers will see significant reductions in the payouts they thought they would receive. So that only leaves the third and final leg—personal savings.

Faced with the daunting possibility of having to rely more and more on personal savings, you will probably consider the usual

Traditional Sources of Retirement Income

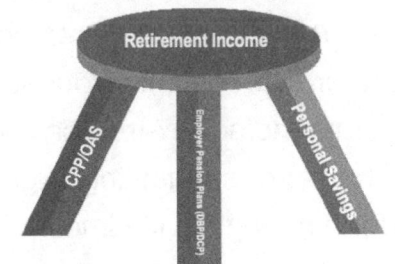

What would happen if one leg was shorter than the other two? The stool, which represents your retirement income, would lack stability.

Source: New York Life Insurance Company

investment options. A Guaranteed Investment Certificate (GIC) may sound like a solid move, for example, since it is CDIC-insured and you can sign up at your local bank. However, we are going to go ahead and put a nail in the GIC coffin for anything other than short-term needs. There is almost no reason for you to invest your hard-earned money in a GIC.

Let's take a closer look at GICs—their interest rates as of late have been nothing short of pathetic. Currently, the average return on a one-year GIC is a measly 1.5%. A two-year GIC? About 2%. Don't spend it all in one place! Money market funds are not faring too much better. Do you know what a typical money market fund is paying? Only 0.1%. That means on a $35,000 balance a money market account pays about $2.92 per month—absolutely ridiculous.

Other alternatives might include stocks, bonds, mutual funds, or ETFs. However, these products bring market risk back into the equation. While that may be fine while you are building your savings, it will not give you much peace of mind if you are taking money out for income during a market crash.

Why Annuities Win Out: Mortality Credits

At this point, we hope, for your sake, that you have limited any major GIC or money market investments your advisors may have offered to short-term needs only. Your accountant or banker may now be recommending tax-free savings accounts, and your stock-broker may be suggesting high dividend-paying stocks. Why settle for a boring old lifetime income annuity when you could buy bonds or stocks instead? To know why, check out the average annuity payout rates of most insurance companies in Canada. Did you know that at age 65, you are guaranteed about 6.15% a year for the rest of your life? At 75, you are guaranteed about 8.25% a year for the rest of your life. And once you reach 85, you are guaranteed almost 12.75% every year for the rest of your life. (Note: these payout rates will change when interest rates change or products are re-priced.)

For those of you who are still more inclined to invest in bank products: do banks offer different interest rates based on age? No, they pay everyone the same rate. As do bonds. Ask your stockbroker: do stocks pay higher dividends based on your age? No!

Issue Age	Annual Payout Rate*
65	6.15%
75	8.25%
85	12.75%

*Sample rates, actual rates may vary

Source: Cannex, 2014.

So here is an important concept to understand: a lifetime income annuity has higher payout rates based on age because the annuity holder gets paid mortality credits. In effect, the main reason you want to buy a lifetime income annuity is because you get paid mortality credits. GICs pay no mortality credits. Bonds pay no mortality credits. Stocks have never paid a mortality credit in the history of the stock market. Lifetime income annuities are structured to satisfy the needs of aging clients, and that is why annuities are the only financial product that offers mortality credits. Dr. Moshe Milevsky, finance professor at the Schulich School of Business at York University in Toronto, refers to these mortality credits as "longevity credits" because you actually get paid for living longer! (See Appendix.)

What are mortality credits, exactly? Basically, they are a financial reward that increases the longer you live. The more years you spend holding a lifetime income annuity, the more mortality credits you will be paid. These have nothing to do with stocks or interest rate returns. Instead, it is an actuarial calculation by the insurance company, based on your age and gender, which adds a credit from the entire risk pool of everyone who buys the same type of lifetime income annuity. This may sound a little confusing, but it really is not. Life insurance companies know when people are going to die. Now, they do not know when you are going to die, but they know almost exactly how long 100 people just like you will live as a group. Because of that, the insurance companies can pay each person as though they knew when each person is going to die. Because some people will die early and will not collect income for that long, they can pay the entire pool a little more than a traditional investment.

We know what some of you are thinking: "What if I'm one of the first ones to go? I don't want my money to disappear when I die." But consider this: does your money have to disappear when you die? Not at all—you can do joint life. Joint life with your spouse, joint life with your kids, joint life with your grandkids. You can choose life with 20 years certain payments, life with 30 years certain payments, life with guaranteed death benefit, or life with cash refund. Less than 10% of lifetime income annuities sold are life-only (the money disappears when you die). Almost everyone wants a guarantee that their money will outlast them somehow. These guarantees are available with annuities, but they will reduce your income payments. The older you are, the longer you live, and the fewer guarantees you choose, the more mortality credits you will be paid and the higher your annual income payment will be.

Goal: Providing Income Across Generations

Tom recently did a seminar at an IMAX Theater in the United States for an audience of about 400 people. When he finished, an 83-year-old gentleman approached him. He said, "Well, Tom, that was a very interesting presentation. But what should I do with my money?" And so Tom asked him two fundamental questions: what do you want your money to do while you're alive, and what do you want it to do when you die? And here's what he said: "Well, I reckon nobody's ever asked me that before. But here's what I want: I want a guaranteed paycheque every month for the rest of my life. And when I die, I want my wife to get that same cheque for the rest of her life. Now when she dies, we want our son to get that same cheque for the rest of his life. And then when he dies, I suppose his wife should get it for the rest of her life. And finally, when his wife dies, we want our granddaughter to get it for the rest of her life. That's what I want." Lucky for him, he can accomplish all of this with just one lifetime income annuity.

Here is how:

1. Joint Annuitants are Grandpa and the grand-daughter.

2. Grandma is named as successor owner.

3. When Grandpa dies, Grandma names the son as the successor owner.

4. When Grandma dies, the son names his wife as the successor owner.

5. When both the husband and wife die, the cheques will go to the granddaughter for the rest of her life.

6. When both Grandpa and the granddaughter die, the cheques will cease.*

*This, of course, assumes that the grand-daughter will live longer than her parents and grandparents. In Canada, the granddaughter would need to be 18 years old or older at the time of purchase.

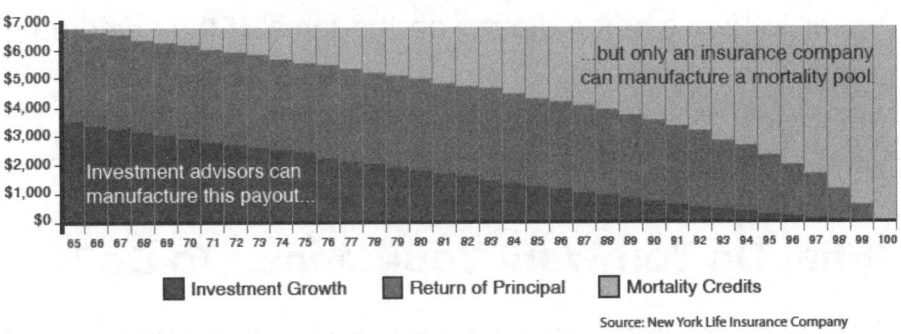

Components of Lifetime Income Payout
Male age 65, $100,000 investment

...but only an insurance company can manufacture a mortality pool

Investment advisors can manufacture this payout...

■ Investment Growth   ■ Return of Principal   □ Mortality Credits

Source: New York Life Insurance Company

There are three parts to a lifetime income annuity pay-cheque. The first part is principal (that is the medium grey in the middle). The second part is interest, which is the lower dark portion. Investment advisors using stock or bond funds can give you both principal and interest. But what they cannot do without an insurance company is pay mortality credits. That is the extra income indicated in the lightest area at the top.

OTHER PEOPLE'S MONEY

Here is another way to think of mortality credits. A financial advisor told us that many of his clients had not saved enough money for retirement. There was no way they could use stocks, bonds, or GICs to withdraw enough money without a high probability of running out of money. He told his clients the best chance they had was to pool their money with a group of other people who also had not saved enough. If they all selected "life-only" pay-outs, the payout rates would be high enough for them to have a decent chance at a successful retirement. As people died, some of their money, in effect, went to those who were still alive. The financial advisor called the mortality credits "other people's money". These people had decided it would be better to "leave some money on the table" if they died early, rather than running out of money while alive. We believe, unfortunately, that many Baby Boomers will find themselves in a similar situation.

What Do You Want Your Money To Do?

Before you can begin planning a successful retirement, you must ask yourself two fundamental questions: (1) what do I need my money to do, and (2) what do I want it to do? As surprising as it may seem, many retirees cannot confidently answer either of these questions.

You need to identify what expenses you have to consider in order to satisfy both your needs and your desires. Then you must consider your options for covering these expenses with guaranteed sources of income.

Know What Your Basic Expenses Are

Luckily, the answer to the first question should be the same for all retirees—you need your money to cover your basic living expenses. We realize these costs are not what most people think about when contemplating retirement. But they are an essential part of a successful retirement plan. What these costs entail will vary for each individual, but will usually comprise a combination of the following:

Housing: Whether you have yet to finish paying off your mortgage or you simply pay rent every month, housing costs can be a significant expense for many retirees. When determining your monthly living cost, be sure to include the money you spend on utilities, internet, television, and upkeep on top of your rent or mortgage payment. If you have been lucky enough to completely pay off your house, you still must consider property taxes and repairs. Do not leave any basic living expenses out of your budget—they are the most important.

Health: It is paramount that you estimate the funds that you will need for prescription drugs, handicapped accommodation, surgeries, and perhaps long-term care. We cannot stress enough that your healthcare costs are expected to rise significantly as you grow older. Setting aside money specifically for health insurance, long-term care insurance, and unexpected events is a must for retirees.

Food and Personal Spending: Figure out how much money you spend monthly on groceries and dining out. You will also want to factor in how much you spend on hygiene products and other amenities—basically everything that you buy and need on a regular basis. Some people spend $200 a week on groceries without even realizing what a large chunk of their budget they are spending.

Transportation: If you do not own a car, transportation costs should hopefully remain quite low (occasional bus, train, or plane fare, but nothing more). Car owners, however, must be wary of the expenses they will continue to incur throughout retirement. These include the skyrocketing price of gas, as well as auto loan and auto insurance payments. Additionally, the sudden need for repairs or maintenance can compound standard transportation costs.

Debt: If you have any outstanding loans—be it anything from your child's college tuition to credit card debt—it is imperative to account for this in your basic expenses budget. You can also look at ways to consolidate debt or reduce interest payments. (If it is paid off by the time you retire, you are fine.)

The Importance of Playcheques

When you think about retirement, what do you usually think of? Some people will say travel. Others will say golf or gardening. Others just want to have time to do all of the things they never had time to do. Most people would probably not say, "Being able to buy groceries or pay my mortgage or pay for health insurance". Paying for basic living expenses is an important step, but it is only the beginning.

This is where the second question comes into play: what do you want your money to do? Once you have retired, there is no more 9-to-5. You are no longer tied to an office five days a week. Every day is Saturday, meaning your number of opportunities to have fun has risen dramatically. How you spend this time, and how you spend your money during this time, is entirely up to you, whether it is spent golfing or traveling or lounging on your porch all day. You need to make allowance for the fun stuff in your retirement plan as well. We call income for these activities "Playcheques".

Guaranteed Sources of Income

Now that you have determined your basic expenses and the amount you will spend on them each month, it is time to figure out how much income you will have. When you get right down to it, retirement planning is a fairly simple equation: make sure your income sources are greater than your expenses. First, you will want to subtract your expected OAS and CPP benefits and (if applicable) pension payments from your monthly costs. In all likelihood, these monthly benefits will not cover all of your projected basic living expenses. Still, if you are lucky enough to receive them, you can use them toward paying down your average monthly costs.

After you account for OAS, CPP and pension benefits, whatever the shortfall is, it will need to come from your retirement savings. What is the best way to pay off these costs each month? Guaranteed Investment Certificates and money market funds are paying less than 3% at the moment, so these surely are not efficient methods to pay for basic expenses. Stocks and bonds are subject to market volatility. They definitely seem like a good way to pay when markets are going up, but they are highly risky since withdrawals lock in losses during down markets. Those who continue to withdraw during a down market will run out of funds most quickly.

What retirees need much more than the above products are guaranteed sources of income on which they can depend every month. In addition to defined benefit pensions, OAS and CPP, it is quite possible that you will need a fourth source of income to cover all of your costs. Here is what you need to do: fill in any shortfalls with a lifetime income annuity from a financially strong insurance company. This strategy will guarantee you steady paycheques for the rest of your life. Remember, you also need to have playcheques to cover the fun stuff beyond the basics. Even if most of your basic expenses are covered by OAS & CPP and pension income, a lifetime income annuity can provide you with a stable source of guaranteed paycheques and playcheques.

Even if you only invested $100,000 into a lifetime income annuity, you could still set yourself up with a dependable monthly cheque and an impressive payout. Add on a 10-year payment guarantee and have that $100,000 guaranteed to pay your beneficiary for up to 10 years in the case of an early death. A cash refund option guarantees that you will get paid for life and your beneficiaries will receive a cash refund of the difference between your investment and the money that you received while alive. Annuities provide flexible options that can be tailored to your investment objectives. Here are some examples of annuities features.

	Annuity for Life		w/ 10-yr Guarantee		w/ Cash Refund	
Buyer	**Monthly Check**	**Payout Rate**	**Monthly Check**	**Payout Rate**	**Monthly Check**	**Payout Rate**
65-yr-old-man	$557	6.7%	$545	6.4%	$492	5.7%
65-yr-old-woman	$505	5.9%	$498	5.8%	$473	5.5%
70-yr-old-man	$642	7.4%	$616	7.1%	$540	6.4%
70-yr-old-woman	$571	6.6%	$557	6.5%	$523	6.1%
75-yr-old-man	$757	8.7%	$706	8.2%	$570	6.6%
75-yr-old-woman	$665	7.7%	$639	7.5%	$560	6.5%

*Sample rates, actual rates may vary

Source: Cannex, 2014

In addition, you need to budget so that you do not spend more than what you have for any particular month. Remember, you have to plan for retirement as if you will live to 100. According to Stats Canada, the number of Canadians living to age 100 or greater increased a whopping 61% between 2001 and 2011.

Optimizing Your Portfolio

Now that you have paycheques and playcheques covering all of your basic expenses, you may be wondering what to do with the rest of your savings. The best strategy here is to optimize your portfolio—but this task is ultimately more complicated than it seems. Everyone optimizes their portfolio differently. Financial services companies have programs that ask 14 simple questions, most along the lines of, "How old are you?" and, "How much do you want to leave to your children?" They then develop a two-page customized portfolio optimization, for which step one is to cover your basic expenses with guaranteed income. Once you have done that, they then advise you to place some money in Canadian stocks, some in U.S. stocks, some money in international stocks, some money in bonds, and some in cash, depending on your specific situation.

And what else? Some more guaranteed lifetime income? Yes! Because here is another fact: the day you retire, you cannot optimize your income without using a lifetime income annuity. Dr. Menahem Yaari proved this back in the 1960s. Dr. Yaari discovered that "only a lifetime income annuity can optimize income over the indefinite period of a human life." (See Appendix.) Let us put that into English for the non-believers still out there. Let's assume that you choose to optimize income in retirement without using a lifetime income annuity. Answer one question: What day will you die? We need to know the month, the day, and the year. Because if you do not know when you are going to die, you cannot optimize income in retirement.

Think about it: if you knew you were going to die tomorrow, you could have a heck of a party tonight. But if you knew you were going to live to 100, you would have to be very careful with your money. Of course, you cannot predict the exact time you will die. But luckily, life insurance companies can conduct actuarial calculations to determine your life expectancy. They do not know when each one of you individually will die, but they do know how long any large group of people will live—almost to the exact day. And because they know how long everyone reading this book is likely to live, they can pay each and every one of you as though they knew exactly when each of you will die. An insurance company can optimize your income in retirement. You cannot do it by yourself. It is a mathematical, scientific, and economic fact.

In addition to optimizing your portfolio for lifetime income, your portfolio also needs to be optimized with a special eye on inflation protection. Commodities, stocks, real estate, mutual funds, and variable annuities are all examples of types of investments that tend to keep up with inflation, although these involve taking some market risks with your assets.

Why such a focus on inflation? Because the lifetime income annuity protects against many of the other risks that retirees face. In a deflationary environment, for instance, a lifetime income annuity is one of the best investments you can make. Your paycheque remains the same while expenses go down each year, giving you a higher annual (real) income. A lifetime income annuity also helps protect against longevity risk, since you receive a paycheque each month no matter how long you live. And lastly, a lifetime income annuity certainly protects you from market risk and withdrawal rate risk. So the major risk that remains is inflation, and a lifetime income annuity is vulnerable to inflation risk. Now, you can purchase an inflation protection rider on a lifetime income annuity and have your paycheque grow by 1% to 5% each year. This is certainly an option. Choosing inflation protection, however, results in a lower paycheque initially—sometimes significantly lower.

Portfolio Optimization in Practice

A more effective method, in our experience, is to cover basic expenses with guaranteed lifetime income and then optimize the portfolio with a special eye on inflation protection. Even conservative investors, who may shy away from commodities, real estate, and stocks, still need to seriously reconsider their aversion to risk. When it comes to inflation, which poses a significant risk to seniors, trying to avoid risk in money market funds, bank accounts, and GICs actually increases the risk of inflation, devastating your retirement income buying power over time. Remember, the CDIC will not insure you against the ravages of inflation!

By allocating a portion of your portfolio toward these inflation sensitive investments, one can optimize their portfolio to protect against inflation, so if inflation occurs, the portfolio will likely rise. When the portfolio rises, you can take some profits and purchase some more guaranteed lifetime income. Over time, markets will go up and down, and when they go up, you have the opportunity to profit and buy more guaranteed income.

So what is the net result of our efforts here? We can act to protect our assets against the ravages of deflation, inflation, hyperinflation, and even a Great Depression. Regardless of what the market does, you now can enjoy peace of mind— knowing that you are in a position to have income to cover expenses no matter what the market is doing.

One last thought—let's say you are not yet convinced that a lifetime income annuity is the mathematical solution for your retirement income. You might prefer stocks, bonds, ETFs, or real estate. But here is the problem: stocks do not know when you are going to die. Neither do bonds, real estate, GICs, or ETFs. So if you invest in any of these to cover your basic expenses, we will make you a promise. You will do one of two things: you will either take out too much money, which may result in running out of money eventually, or you will take out too little and forfeit the retirement you could have had.

We know so many seniors who refuse to touch their money. These people are living a "just in case" retirement and never fully enjoy the fruits of all of their labors. Covering your basic expenses with guaranteed lifetime income and optimizing the rest of your portfolio with inflation in mind are the keys to a happy and successful retirement.

Guaranteed Paycheques and Playcheques

 Key Points from Chapter 3

1. A lifetime income annuity is a MUST for an optimal retirement.

2. When every day is Saturday, you'll also need a guaranteed PLAYCHEQUE!

3. GICs were never made for income.

4. It's all about the mortality credits. Because longevity risk multiplies all of the other risks, you HAVE to have mortality credits in your portfolio.

5. Know the difference between your needs and wants in retirement.

6. Cover your basic expenses with guaranteed lifetime income.

7. Optimize your portfolio with a special eye on inflation. Even conservative investors need exposure to investments that will protect them from inflation.

Chapter 4

Investments: Protecting and Optimizing Your Principal

There are so many different types of investment options available today: mutual funds, segregated funds, exchange traded funds, stocks, bonds, guaranteed investment certificates, exempt market products, and hedge funds, to name a few. How do you choose the right type of investment? We will break down some of the options available to you, and focus on investments that provide value-added options, such as guarantees and tax efficiency.

The Best Kept Canadian Secret: Segregated Funds!

Canada is home to the segregated fund, one of the best-kept investment secrets around. Segregated Funds (typically called "Seg Funds") are investments that act like a mutual fund, but are offered by an insurance company and come with guarantees. Seg Funds can have several advantages over mutual funds in certain situations. When we ask people if they have heard of or used Segregated Funds as an investment option, most people say, "Nope, never." Seg Funds aren't new, the market for Seg Funds isn't small, and they have not performed poorly. So why haven't you heard of them?

Marketing. We bet you have never seen an advertisement for a Segregated Fund—anywhere. This lack of marketing may have you thinking that the amount of Seg Funds sold in Canada must be insignificant; again, it's not. The Seg Fund market in Canada has been around for nearly 50 years and the total amount of money invested into Seg Funds is now over $90 billion.

The popularity of Seg Funds took off in the late 90s. This increase in popularity was due to the fact that successful mutual fund managers started working with insurance companies on their segregated fund offerings. This increased the profile and returns of segregated funds and also increased the number of funds being offered. For investors of Segregated Funds, this meant being offered more flavours than simply chocolate or vanilla. Now there was a flavour for everyone.

Segregated Funds offer several distinct advantages over mutual funds:

- Guarantees of principal on maturity and death Potential creditor protection for individuals and business owners

• Simplified estate planning techniques

We will explain all of these advantages in detail.

The selection of available Seg Funds is vast and contains a large assortment of the following types of funds: bond funds, balanced funds, Canadian equity funds and even international equity funds. In fact, a lot of the most popular mutual funds can be purchased as Seg Funds.

For clarity, we are not saying that mutual funds are bad or irrelevant or that Segregated Funds are better. However, in certain circumstances, Segregated Funds are more beneficial to their owners than mutual funds. Both types of investments have their place and we will discuss them in this chapter.

Segregated Fund Ownership

We will get into a few specific examples of how Seg Funds can be set up but we wanted to give you the main players involved in a Seg Fund contract first:

- Owner
- Contingent Owner
- Annuitant
- Beneficiary
- Contingent Beneficiary

The owner of a Seg Fund contract is the person who is investing the money and has control over the account. They can also have contingent owners. This means that if the original owner passes away, it becomes the property of the contingent owner; there would be no probate, no courts involved, and no Will would be necessary to transfer that particular asset. The contract stays intact; the only change is that the owner has been replaced. This is very similar to owning an investment in joint ownership with another person, but there is no need to give any amount of ownership away while the original owner is still alive.

The annuitant is the person to whom all the guarantees are attached and the life that the contract is based on. In most cases, the annuitant is the owner of the Seg Fund, but in certain cases the annuitant can be someone other than the owner, as long as they are not a beneficiary. This is because you cannot insure your life and expect to receive money when you pass away.

The next person, or people, involved in a Seg Fund contract would be those who are entitled to the proceeds of the investment, if there is no contingent owner named. These people are known as beneficiaries, and they receive the proceeds of the account typically within 30 days of the Seg Fund owner's passing. The owner can name as many beneficiaries as they like. There can even be contingent beneficiaries, so if a beneficiary passes away, the portion of the investment that was earmarked for them can be paid out to someone else.

Guaranteed to Not Lose money

Guarantee of principal, or the risk of not losing any of your money, is one of the benefits offered to you when you invest in a Segregated Fund. There are two different types of guarantees offered: a maturity guarantee and a death benefit guarantee. In defining the guarantees of Segregated Funds, both the death benefit guarantee and the maturity guarantee cover only what you originally invested. You also have the choice of guaranteeing 75% or 100% of your original investment. These guarantees do not include any amount that you withdraw or redeem from the fund.

For example, if you invested $25,000 into a fund, and the value of the fund was only $15,000 when you died, and you never redeemed any money from the account, your named beneficiary would receive the $25,000 that you had originally invested. If, on the other hand, you invested $25,000 and the value of the fund was only $15,000 when you passed away, but you had redeemed $10,000 to buy a new car, your named beneficiary would only receive the $15,000.

The contracts for Segregated Funds differ between companies but generally follow guidelines similar to the following:

- Most companies allow for unlimited deposits if the accounts are created before the investor turns 80.

- Some companies cut off all deposits at age 80.

- Some companies offer their funds to investors up to age 90, but the death benefit guarantees are reduced to 75% or 80% of the initial investment.

Segregated Funds are an integral part of any estate plan because of the security they provide. We have dealt with many individuals who recognized the importance of Seg Funds but were beyond the maximum age requirement to invest.

With the maturity guarantee you have the choice when you create the account to protect either 75% of 100% of your original investment. After a predetermined amount of time, if the value of your account is less than what you had originally invested, you have the option of cashing in the account and getting your initial investment back. The maturity guarantee provides the peace of mind of knowing that your initial investment is never at risk of decreasing over the long-term.

While it may seem like there have been very few investments over a 10-to-15-year period that have actually decreased in value, it has happened. One instance that sticks in our minds is an example of how well a Seg Fund worked in 2010. The original Seg Fund purchase occurred back in 2000 before the tech bubble burst, but 2010 was the year that the maturity guarantee kicked in, making for some very happy investors.

Back in early 2000, pretty much everyone was investing in technology dot-com stocks and making a bundle of money. There were mutual funds and Segregated Funds that specialized in the sector and invested heavily in technology. Most of these technology stocks and technology funds lost a large amount of their value, and did so permanently. However, in 2010, the maturity guarantee for Seg Funds purchased in 2000 kicked in. If you were heavily invested in technology-based Seg Funds during the dot-com boom, and lost most of it when the tech bubble burst, in 2010 you would have received your original investment from 10 years ago. Would you have liked the opportunity to get your money back, even if it was a decade after the fact? We don't think that there are many people who would say "No".

Here is the example that we like to use: back in 1999, three brothers bet the farm, and invested all of their money in technology right before the tech bubble burst in 2000. One brother invested everything in technology stocks, the second brother invested everything in technology-based mutual funds, and the third brother invested everything in technology-based segregated funds. Granted, it would be a lean 10 years for the third brother, but we're guessing that after the maturity guarantee kicked in, he would have hosted his other brothers for Thanksgiving at his house in 2009 and probably every year since.

High watermarks, or resets, are also common with Segregated Funds. A reset is when you can reset the maturity guarantee at a new, higher dollar amount. If you had invested $100,000 into a Seg Fund and one year later it was worth $150,000, you could trigger a reset. This would reset both the death benefit guarantee and the maturity guarantee at $150,000. This reset would guarantee that you or your beneficiaries would receive a minimum of $150,000, not $100,000. These resets can be done anywhere from daily, annually, or once every three years. It all depends on the contract.

Segregated Funds, as an Estate Planning vehicle

Earlier we discussed the death benefit guarantee and we mentioned that if you passed away while the value of your Segregated Fund was less than what you originally invested, your named beneficiary would receive the guaranteed value. Unlike mutual funds, stocks, bonds, or any other investment product in Canada, Seg Funds can have named beneficiaries for non-registered investment accounts. This means that any money you have invested in a Seg Fund (that is not held in a registered account such as an RRSP, spousal RRSP, RRIF, LIF, LRIF or TFSA) can have a named beneficiary and the money will go directly to that person.

This benefit of having a named beneficiary is due to the fact that the segregated fund is actually an insurance contract; it falls under the insurance act but is not a life insurance policy. Since Seg Funds are an insurance product, when the investor who owns the Seg Fund passes away, the money goes directly to the named beneficiary (or multiple beneficiaries).

If set up correctly, money invested in a Seg Fund stays outside of the estate, and therefore bypasses probate. While probate in some provinces can be a fixed rate as low as $400, it can also be as high as a 1.5% fee or tax on every asset held in an estate. The 1.5% probate fee can get expensive.

If you had $1,000,000 invested and you passed away, the probate tax or fee could be as high as $15,000, depending on which province you live in. This is $15,000 that your estate would not have to pay, had you invested that money in a Segregated Fund. Do you think that the $15,000 would have been of benefit to a grandchild or a great grandchild? The $15,000 could have been invested and used for a few years of university, paid for a year at private school, or been donated to your favourite charity. Instead, the $15,000 went to your provincial government.

Taxes play a positive, significant role in helping us to live the lifestyle we have all grown accustomed to. However, if your intention was to provide a portion of the value of your estate to your provincial government, you would have named the provincial government as the designated beneficiary of your Seg Fund. If you had done this, you could have saved the province the administration fee and court costs of dealing with your estate by having it bypass probate. In Ontario and BC, where probate fees are among the highest in the country, you can save your estate and your beneficiaries a lot of money by using segregated funds.

On top of saving probate fees, when money is paid out of a Seg Fund, it is private transaction and is incontestable. This means no one can dispute the decision of the person who established the account (unlike a will, which is public record and contestable). A private, incontestable payout normally occurs within 30 days after the date of the annuitant's death. By all accounts, is better than the months or even years it can take to work their way through the courts.

If a person passes away without a valid will, then the process of settling their estate will take even longer. We would like to point out that no funds are paid from an estate that is still before the courts. No beneficiary of a will receives any inheritance until the estate has been settled with probate being assessed and paid.

When it comes to estate planning, Segregated Funds take an enormous burden off of an executor. If you have ever been an executor of an estate, you know that it is hard, time-consuming work during a very difficult and emotional time. For those who have never had the trusted misfortune of being an executor, all you have to know is that it can be one of the most stressful and thankless jobs around.

Seg Funds simplify the process of settling an estate. In the eyes of the provincial government, any money invested in a Seg Fund does not form a part of your estate. This means that if all of your assets are invested in a Seg Fund, it is possible that you will not need a will. Since there is no will, there are no lawyers involved and no probate courts to work through. No probate and no lawyers means no fees and no probate taxes. In the end, the beneficiary will receive their portion of assets within 30 days and only the advisor, the insurance company, and the beneficiary will know that they received anything, guaranteeing that your money went to the person or people you wanted.

Protected from Creditors

If Segregated Funds are set up correctly from the beginning, individuals can possess the ability to have their money protected from creditors. If you get sued or go bankrupt, and if the purpose of investing in a Seg Fund was not just to shelter your money from a pending bankruptcy, there is a very good chance that no one will be able to take your money from you. This is especially relevant to asset protection and retirement planning for business owners and professionals.

Could you imagine working your entire career, owning your own business or professional practice, and then losing your business and all of your personal savings because you or someone in your organization made a mistake? That would be devastating; you would lose your entire retirement nest egg and your life's work. If you had your savings in a Segregated Fund though, your assets could have been protected and your retirement would have remained intact. It's that simple.

Another way we explain the value of the creditor-protection offered by a Seg Fund is during the transfer of wealth, or at inheritance time. Most likely, we all know someone who has an adult child who may not be the best with money, who has either declared bankruptcy (or is close to it), or who is simply not able to make sound financial decisions on their own. Segregated Funds can be used to ensure that the money that was saved and put aside to look after the dependent person is not taken by someone else and that the money is used specifically for the best interest of the dependent person.

When it comes to estate planning, Seg Funds are essential. If you're still not convinced, let's take a look at an example.

A couple in their 70s had a son who was unable to make sound financial decisions on his own. He had declared bankruptcy and was constantly in financial trouble. This, in turn, made his parents feel that it would be impossible to leave him with a lump sum of money after they had both passed away. The couple spoke with their lawyer and they all decided that a trust should be set up for their son. This would ensure that their money could be paid monthly out of the trust to fund the living expenses of their child for as long as there was money in the trust. It would also guarantee that potential future creditors would not be able to access his inheritance while the money was invested in the trust.

The costs to set up and maintain a trust like the one the couple wanted can be significant. On top of the cost, a trustee has to maintain the investments, making sure that the inheritance for the couple's son was invested prudently, which either meant that the inheritance would earn very low return or that it would be exposed to market risk. Setting up a trust is a common solution that many lawyers and individuals settle on.

The couple met with their lawyer, paying $1000 to redo their wills and have a testamentary trust created (which is created from the will, after both the husband and wife have passed away). After the trust is set up, every year the trust has money in it, the trust will have to file a separate tax return because it is taxed as a separate entity. When the parents pass away, a trustee is instructed to pay a monthly amount to their child for as long as he lives or as long as there is money in a trust. The trust is contestable, though; the couple's son could challenge the fairness of the trust in court and seek a lump sum of money or even the payout of the trust in its entirety.

If the couple had been aware of all of their options, they would come to us. While setting up a trust is the common method, we may have suggested an alternative that could work better for everyone involved, except perhaps the lawyer and the accountant.

We would have had the couple put the money into a Seg Fund. This would have provided them with the guarantee that, at a minimum, the amount they invested would be transferred to their son. The Segregated Fund, after their deaths, would have instructions to purchase an indexed annuity with their son named as the beneficiary of that annuity. Using a Seg Fund allows the couple to maintain control of their money during their lifetime and after their passing. A trust can be contested and, more often than you would think, they are. The Seg Fund annuity option cannot be contested. When the last one of them passes away, the money remains outside of their will, bypassing probate, and directly purchasing an indexed annuity for their son. This would provide their son with an increasing revenue stream for every year of his life,taking away the risk that he would ever outlive the money his parents set aside for him. It would ensure that the transfer of his inheritance to the annuity and the proceeds from the annuity would be creditor-protected, no one would ever be able to take his monthly income from him.

If the couple's son had children, an annuity could have been purchased that would provide the couple's grandchildren with a lump sum or another annuity if their son had passed away before using up the entire principal from his annuity. This provides a tremendous opportunity for providing your loved ones with security.

The best part about this concept: no set up or maintenance fees. Compared to the $1000 that it would have cost to create the trust in the first place, the couple and their son are already ahead. Since no trust was created, there is no annual accounting or trustee expenses, and because the Seg Fund transferred the couple's money outside of the estate upon their last death, there were no probate costs. The most important part of this whole process is that the couple knew the minimum amount that their son would be getting. They also knew that their son would never run the risk of outliving the money they had set aside for him. Seg Funds simplify difficult situations.

You Get What You Pay For

A common criticism of Seg Funds is that they can be expensive from a management fee perspective. While Seg Fund fees can be slightly higher than mutual fund fees, the benefits and guarantees offset the increased management expense. A portfolio offered as a Segregated Fund, with a value of less than $250,000, will typically have a higher fee. The fees we are talking about are management fees, also known as the management expense ratio, which is the fee that you pay for having a team of professionals manage your money.

With Segregated Funds you get what you pay for. The benefits of principal guarantees, creditor protection, and estate planning efficiency offered in a Segregated Fund may be worth the increased fee to the right person.

The relevance of a Segregated Fund in an individual's portfolio is a question for the individual and their advisor; unfortunately, not all advisors have this conversation with their clients. Seg Funds may not be suitable for everyone but they are a wonderful solution for almost every person. Questions like, "how am I going to make sure my money goes where I want it to when I die?" and "how do I ensure that my wishes are followed after I am gone?" can be answered with certainty when using Seg Funds because of their benefits.

For Seg Fund portfolios with a value greater than $250,000, the management fee is typically reduced to a very low number. With several insurance companies, the management fee is reduced to well below the fee charged by an average mutual fund. This reduction of Seg Fund management fees makes the Seg Fund a better overall performer than a comparable mutual fund even without the added benefits of the Seg Fund. The companies that offer a reduction in management fees typically have their own investment management team and do not outsource portfolio management.

Term Deposits Invested with Insurance Companies

For individuals who are looking for a short-term investment with a guaranteed rate of return, we frequently suggest an investment similar to a GIC, but offered by an insurance company. These term deposits have several different names: Guaranteed Income Options (GIO), Guaranteed Income Accounts (GIA), or as we refer to them: "term funds". The most typical investment lengths for term funds are 1-5 years, like GICs. However, GIC terms are usually non-redeemable, meaning that once you choose this investment, your money is locked in for the length of the term. Term funds, though, are redeemable (with a possible penalty or other type of market value adjustment).

Term funds offer the same guarantees and protection offered in a Seg Fund, but with guaranteed rates of return for fixed amounts of time, like GICs. This makes them very safe and very efficient, from investment and estate planning perspectives. The term fund option is also a very good tool when a person is in their 80s or 90s and is interested in estate planning but unable to purchase a typical Seg Fund, due to their age.

The rate of return on term funds offered by an insurance company are quite comparable to the rate of return offered by traditional GICs. This is interesting, considering that the term funds can be creditor-protected if the owner of the term deposit declares bankruptcy. In addition, if the owner passes away, the money will go directly to named beneficiaries and bypass probate.

Too often, we are visited by elderly individuals holding GICs in joint name with one or more of their children; they do this in order to make the estate wealth transfer more effective. What these people and their advisors may be overlooking is that while this solution does bypass probate, it is not without inefficiencies, risks, and inconveniences. Lots of us have parents who may be getting on in age, who might be looking for easy ways to transfer their wealth. If you have elderly parents, or you are looking for something better than joint ownership of investment GICs, then you will hopefully find this information of great use.

When you hold a GIC in joint name with an adult child, that GIC investment is now legally owned by both of you. As the original owner, you have given away ownership of half of that investment. Since half is owned by you and half is owned by someone else, if either of you were to get into financial trouble, there is the possibility that 100% of that investment could be seized.

Estate planning via joint ownership will therefore increase the risk of having your money seized, even if both owners are responsible and have never had any money trouble. An example we like to use is Mrs. Smith, who is 90 years old, and her 60-year-old daughter Karen, who is now joint owner of what used to be solely her mother's GIC portfolio. Karen's husband owns a very successful business; they live very comfortably and have never had any financial problems. However, if Karen and her husband do run into money problems for any reason, either personally or because of their business, the creditors could come after Mrs. Smith's GICs. While the chances of Karen and her husband running in to money problems may be low, is it worth the unnecessary risk?

GICs that are jointly owned are not wound-down when one of the owners passes away. Using the example of Mrs. Smith and Karen again, this time we find out that Mrs. Smith has two other children who, because they live in other cities, are not named as joint owners. Karen has said that she will disperse the money after her mother passes away, but the GIC terms are invested equally into terms spread out over the next five years. If Mrs. Smith passes away tomorrow, it will take five years for her children to receive their inheritance. Meanwhile, Karen will have to pay tax on all the interest earned in the GICs over that time span. Since the GICs do not pay out on the death of the first joint owner, they are not ideal for transferring money through joint ownership.

If Mrs. Smith had invested her money in a term fund instead of GICs, she would be the sole owner of the term fund account. Even if she was sued or she ran into money problems, it is likely that creditors would not be able to seize these term funds because of the protection offered by Seg Funds. She would also have the ability to name her three children as equal beneficiaries, and the proceeds of the account would bypass probate and could pay out within 30 days of her passing, provided that the proper documentation was made available. This way, Karen would not have to pay tax on the interest, and all of Mrs. Smith's children would receive their inheritance much sooner.

Term funds offer a great solution to investors who do not want to take on any risk, want to preserve the value of their investments, and are interested in an efficient and economical estate transfer process.

Investment Options: You Can't Have Your Cake and Eat it, Too

There is no such thing as the perfect investment; investments cannot be all things to all people, or even all things to one person. There are investments that are suited to most situations, but not every situation at once. You have to make trade-offs depending on what your priorities are. This is especially true when you are looking for an investment that gives you protection, tax-efficiency, guaranteed principal, and easy accessibility to your money, while at the same time providing the opportunity for capital appreciation.

Throughout this book, we will look at several different investment vehicles: annuities, participating whole life insurance, segregated funds, and term funds. All of these investments offer varying degrees of safety, security, and guarantees, while providing the potential for growth. We are going to change gears now and discuss investments that have been created for higher potential returns and tax efficiency (rather than guarantees of income or principal). Exchange Traded Funds (ETFs) and Mutual Funds are two investments that are centred around these attributes.

ETFs: The New Kids on the Block

Exchange Traded Funds (ETFs) are a relatively new type of investment and hold a collection of investments, like a mutual fund or a Segregated Fund. ETFs can hold stock, bonds or commodities, we are going to be discussing ETFs that hold stocks and track an index. The most common type of ETF is a weighted representation of an index. That may be Greek to most of you, but it means that all ETFs follow a specific group of stocks; no one picks which stocks are included or which stocks are excluded. They are all included.

Some stocks or publically-traded companies, like Tim Horton's, TD Canada Trust, and Potash Corp, are traded on the Toronto Stock Exchange (TSX). Each company mentioned also makes up a part of the S&P TSX Composite Index. The S&P TSX Composite Index is an average of the largest stocks traded on the TSX according to market capitalization (company size). Each of these companies also belongs to a different sector or industry in the Canadian economy, making it easy to identify other companies in the same business or industry. TD Canada Trust, for example, is traded on the TSX. TD is also part of the financial sector of the Canadian economy, which means that its stock is included in the TSX Composite Index and is part of the Canadian Financial Sector index. Other bank and insurance company stocks are also included in both indexes. An index is simply a collection of stocks with something in common. Another example of an index is the S&P 500 in the United States. For more information on the Toronto Stock Exchange, please go to their website at www.TMX.com.

Low fees and modern portfolio theory were the inspiration for the creation of ETFs. Modern portfolio theory is the belief that, over the long-term, no person or group of people can consistently beat the market. With no active supervision or stock-picking in an attempt to achieve positive results, ETFs are considered a passive investment strategy.

The term "passive" means that the stocks are left to their own devices. This results in less risk of human error. The markets, in theory, will provide the best possible return. ETFs have very low management fees; this is because no one is actually picking the stocks or actively managing the fund for the investors. Why pay someone to manage something that doesn't need much managing? The lower fee is one of the ways to achieve a higher rate of return. However, we repeat the old adage: "You get what you pay for." You may pay less in fees for limited active money management, but you get potentially less tax efficiency and no guarantees or estate transfer benefits in return.

Tax Strategies for Your Non-registered Portfolio

We are going to discuss how certain mutual funds can provide for tax-efficient growth and tax-deferred distributions. Seg Funds offer guarantees, protection of capital and estate planning benefits; ETFs provide very low fees; certain mutual funds can provide active management and tax efficiency for non-registered accounts. This type of fund offers tax-deferred growth in the accumulation phase, and tax-deferred trading and withdrawals later on when you start using your savings as income.

Most advisors in the mutual fund business use a lot of jargon with funny names for complicated products and concepts. The concepts themselves aren't difficult, but what they are called does not seem to coincide with what the funds actually do. Don't worry. We'll give you the industry jargon name first, so that when you are meeting with your advisor you'll be able to talk the talk and walk the walk. After the first time, we'll use a more descriptive name (and stick with it), which will help the concept make sense to you.

The concepts we are going to discuss here are tax-deferral concepts, not tax avoidance or strategies for tax evasion. To paraphrase Ben Franklin: at the end of the day, there are two things you can count on...death and taxes. For most of us, we will have no control over when we die, so let's leave that for the life insurance companies to worry about. Instead, we'll focus on the one thing that, to a certain extent, we can control: deferring taxes.

Certain types of mutual funds can defer tax while you accumulate money, allowing for compounded growth by limiting the interest and dividend income that flows into the fund. This is similar to the benefits offered in an RRSP or a TFSA, but it is available, to a certain extent, in non-registered mutual funds.

We'll explain how these types of funds will also let you switch holdings within your account, without paying any tax on any gains you have made. You will be able to sell and buy funds within your account without worrying about those taxes.

These same mutual funds can be set up so that you pay less in fees and allow for tax-advantaged withdrawals. These withdrawals can systematically provide you with a set amount of income per month, so that you may not have to pay any tax for many years.

The three types of mutual funds that we are going to discuss are: Corporate Class, T-series and F-Class. There they are, in all their splendour and glory. Given those titles, would you be able to tell us what they do for you and how they provide a value added in your portfolio? Probably not, and that's okay. You'll soon be able to.

Benefits of Corporate Class Funds

Corporate Class mutual funds provide the owners of non-registered investments the ability for some tax-deferred growth. This type of tax-deferred growth, typically found in an RRSP or a TFSA, is available to certain non-registered investments.

Quick history lesson—previously, mutual funds were set up as mutual fund "trusts". Today, many mutual funds are set up as a mutual fund "corporation". By having mutual funds set up as a corporation, the mutual fund companies are able to provide much greater tax efficiency for the investors. The increased tax efficiency of having investments held in a mutual fund corporation is due to the fact that distributions (interest and dividends earned within the investment) flowing into the fund are limited. The majority of the growth, or increase in the value of the fund, is largely attributed to capital gains, which is more tax-efficient.

You can buy and sell mutual funds held in a mutual fund corporation and not pay any capital gains when you switch from one fund to another fund. This strategy works well as you get older, because you can gradually make your portfolios safer by increasing bonds and fixed income investments while reducing the amount of stocks you hold. Also, it can be done without paying tax on any capital gains, potentially allowing for much higher long-term returns. This type of deferral is one of the major benefits of RRSPs, but can now be accomplished in non-registered portfolios.

Wouldn't it be great to avoid paying tax on a non-registered portfolio over a 20-year period, buying and selling different mutual funds along the way? It certainly would! By deferring the tax during those 20 years, you would end up with a lot more money; this is a fact.

Mutual funds held in a mutual fund corporation are definitely better for accumulating assets, but will they help in retirement? Long story short, owning corporation-held mutual funds will only help from a tax-deferral perspective, there are no specific advantages to owning them while you are redeeming money in lump sums. If you want to redeem your money in a systematic way over time, then a certain type of mutual fund held in a mutual fund corporation could help defer tax on your withdrawals as well. These types of funds are called Tax Series funds.

Tax Efficient Withdrawals from Tax Series Funds

Tax series funds (also called "T-Series") provide tax efficient income, which can be beneficial for new retirees. Typically, the first few years of retirement are the most active for new retirees. They do a lot of travelling and take up new hobbies, and, as a result, they spend a lot of money. Since retirement is basically a very long vacation, it can become an expensive twilight career. Without jobs to provide a source of income for that increased spending, retirees need to make sure that they have enough sustainable income available to them. The more tax efficient that income is, the better.

Increasing taxable income in retirement has the potential to jeopardize the Old Age Security (OAS) pension, in the form of OAS clawbacks. Increasing taxable income will also result in more taxes owed and potentially higher tax rates. As you take more money out of your portfolio, your assets will decrease and the government's income will increase. Ideally, the income that you take in retirement should have an em- phasis on being tax-efficient.

There are mutual funds that allow for tax-deferred withdrawals. This is not an option with ETFs or stock and bond portfolios; only annuities or permanent life insurance can offer similar tax-deferred income to these types of mutual funds. However, these mutual funds do not come with income guarantees or mortality credits. Since these mutual funds do not have guarantees, you are at risk of eventually running out of money.

We spoke about mutual funds held in a corporation and their ability to provide tax-deferred growth—now let's talk about tax-deferred withdrawals. This is where you withdraw money from your non-registered investment accounts and pay limited tax on what you take out of that account for many years. These investments are held in a corporate mutual fund, allowing for tax-deferred growth, and can be called T-Series, T-SWIP, or tax-efficient mutual funds.

The thinking behind tax-efficient mutual funds is that they allow for tax-deferred income in retirement, which can play an important part in everyone's retirement income strategy. As we mentioned earlier, the first 10 years of retirement tend to be expensive (Every day is Saturday!), where travelling and hobbies become a new career. For people who require some income from their mutual fund portfolio, we often recommend this strategy. These mutual funds work by providing income that is considered a mixture of return of capital and income earned from dividends and interest.

Return of capital refers to the money you originally invested. You do not have to pay any tax on this money when it is taken out of an investment portfolio. Eventually, you will have taken out all of your original investment, and future redemptions could be considered capital gains, which will be taxed. This strategy would be most appropriate for providing income early on in retirement, when you will be spending more money.

Tax-efficient mutual funds provide a fixed amount of income on a monthly basis, typically 5% or 8% of the portfolio, paid out equally over 12 months. The amount paid out is based on total value of the account on January 1st of each year. If the mutual fund has a return that is greater than the 5% or 8% being withdrawn annually, the account will increase in value. If the investment return is less than the amount being withdrawn on a consistent basis, your account will eventually run out of money.

The sequence of return risk we discussed earlier in the book is a risk with tax series mutual funds, but you can start and stop the payments whenever you choose. This is the trade-off you need to consider between a flexible, tax-efficient mutual fund and the tax efficiency and guaranteed income from an annuity. In many cases, a combination of the two allow for flexibility, convenience, and security.

Earlier on, we looked at the amount of income you could withdraw from your portfolio in order to guarantee that you would never run out of money. It certainly wasn't 8% or even 5%; it was more like 2%. This leads us to the belief that while tax-efficient mutual funds are convenient for providing tax-deferred income in the short-term, they are not the best solution for providing long-term income. Since the 5% or 8% withdrawal rate is historically proven to be unsustainable and an annuity can provide guaranteed returns in excess of 5%, annuities are the best long-term choice for guaranteed retirement income. Over the short-term, though, particularly in the early years of retirement, a tax-efficient mutual fund can provide for tax-deferred income while new retirees are spending more money. This will keep money invested in the market and allow for easy access to capital for one-time expenses or emergencies. It also provides an income stream that can be turned on or off at any time, in addition to possessing limited tax consequences.

Tax-efficient mutual funds can provide an excellent source of income for your Playcheque.

Transparency & Tax Deductions

There are two ways that Canadians pay for investment advice involving mutual funds and Seg Funds. The different ways to pay for money management are the Management Expense Ratio (MER) structure and a fee-based structure.

The MER structure is the most common form of paying for a mutual fund or Seg Fund and is the default option for most advisors. If you are not sure which payment structure arrangement you have with your advisor, just ask. With this form of payment, the fee that is charged is an embedded payment. You don't physically pay the fee; it is taken directly from the fund you are invested in. The returns that you see on your annual statement are all after the fees are paid. The MER taken from the fund provides the portfolio managers and your financial advisors with monthly income in return for supervising your funds and accounts. The transparency (or lack thereof) of the embedded-fee option is being hotly debated lately by proponents of full disclosure.

The fee-based structure is made up of two parts. The first part is where the mutual fund charges you a reduced management fee to pay for their administration, portfolio management, legal fees, and other expenses they need to incur to keep the lights on and turn a profit. The second part of the fee is a negotiated fee that you pay your advisor. The fee is set each year, and is normally paid monthly. The fee is a percentage of the total assets that you have invested with your advisor. The typical annual fee is about 1%, but can be increased or decreased depending on the size of your portfolio. In both the MER structure and the fee-based model, if your portfolio dropped 30%, as it most likely did in 2008, then your advisor's income decreased by 30%. Their success is tied to your success in both cases. The fee-based structure is not an embedded fee, however, you either use cash that is in your portfolio, you sell a portion of your investments, or you write your advisor a cheque. This model is actually how most of the world pays for financial advice, not the embedded structure that exists in Canada.

Having to pay for advice may seem like an increased amount of work on your end, rather than simply having the mutual fund companies take care of it. However, like most things, if something takes a bit more effort, it may be worth it in the long run. Specifically in the case of non-registered portfolios, we feel that it is probably worth the time and effort.

One of the advantages of using the fee-based structure for your mutual fund portfolios is that the total amount of fees paid, including the amount negotiated with your advisor, may be less than what is paid when using the MER structure. Since reducing fees is one of the only guaranteed ways to make more money, fee-based accounts have the potential to increase your net worth and the size of a portfolio over the long-term.

The second advantage is only available when investing in a non-registered or open portfolio. The fee that you pay your advisor is tax-deductible, if you are in a high enough tax bracket. This will result in a reduction of net fees paid. If you negotiate a 1% management fee with your advisor and you are in a 40% tax bracket, after deductions, this brings your management fee down to 0.60%. This leaves even more money in your pocket at the end of the day, which, when you're retired, means more security.

A lot of advisors in Canada are hesitant to move to a fee-based model because they are afraid that their clients will resent having to write a cheque in a down year. Advisors feel that if their clients had a $250,000 portfolio and the advisor charged a 1% fee for a total of $2,500, how happy would the client be if another year like 2008 happened again? Their portfolio has just dropped by 30% from $250,000 to $175,000, but they still need to pay their advisor $2,500. They wouldn't be too happy… even though, moving forward, they would only have to pay $1,750 because the advisor's pay would have decreased by 30% as well. The fact is that you are already paying these fees; it simply depends on whether or not you want to pay attention to what you are paying.

A fee-based structure may be a very good option for non-registered mutual fund accounts and can also make sense when it comes to registered portfolios. Our reasoning is that one of the few ways to consistently earn a higher rate of return over the long-term is through consistently paying less in fees. Mutual funds held in a corporation can also be set up using the fee-based structure, which creates tax deferral and tax deduction options.

Mutual Funds Summary

The types of mutual funds that we have mentioned, offer tax deferral strategies that are not available in other types of investments, but they are not without risk. There is no such thing as the perfect investment. There is always a trade-off between tax efficiency, guarantees, liquidity, growth, and income. A combination of different types of investments allows you to optimize the potential from your investments.

Investments: Protecting and Optimizing Your Principal

 Key Points from Chapter 4

1. Segregated Fund benefits: Maturity guarantee of your principal, death benefit guarantee of your principal, creditor protection of your investments, incontestable payout to beneficiaries that by-passes probate, and not to mention the allowable resets that can increase your guaranteed amount.

2. You get what you pay for. For accounts over $250,000, there is a decent chance that segregated management fees will be less than conventional mutual fund fees. For accounts under $250,000, the benefits offered by a Segregated Fund may offset the slight increase in fees.

3. There is no such thing as the perfect investment. There are investments that offer principal protection, estate planning benefits, tax efficiency, income, or growth; work with your advisor choosing the investment or combination of investments that will help you to achieve your goals.

4. Corporate Class mutual funds can help you to defer tax which can result in more savings at the end of the day.

5. Tax Series mutual funds can provide income for your Playcheque and could be a great, tax efficient source of income earlier on in retirement while you may be more active.

Chapter 5

Customized Solutions to Everyday Retirement Problems

As the sun sets on your career and every day is about to become Saturday, you will be faced with issues such as: how to effectively take your required minimum withdrawals from your Registered Retirement Income Fund (RRIF) after you have converted your RRSP; when to start taking the Canada Pension Plan; how the government pensions CPP & Old Age Security (OAS) payments are taxed; Is the OAS clawback as painful as it sounds?; how to recover from a bear (negative) market; what the Tax-Free Savings Account is and why you should have one; good alternatives to low-yielding GICs or savings accounts; and how you can come up with a creative way to provide yourself with a guaranteed income stream for life and also leave a legacy to your children, grandchildren and great-grandchildren.

RRSPs, RRIFs, and Annuities

Starting at the end of the year in which you turn 71, you have to convert your RRSP into a RRIF. This means that you will have to start taking out a required minimum amount the next year at age 72. This percentage increases gradually until you are 94 when it jumps up to 20% per year, levels off and continues indefinitely until the account is depleted. While the increase each year seems gradual, the eventual outcome is that you will face a significant decrease in income each year because the forced withdrawal rates will eventually become larger than the potential returns of your portfolio and you will be eroding your principal. This means that you will be forced to withdraw your money at an increasing rate, and that the pool from which you are withdrawing from will get smaller and smaller.

Let's take a look at Betty, who is in great health and turned 94 this year. Betty still has $50,000 in a RRIF, which was inherited from her deceased husband. Because of Betty's age and her limited income, her RRIF is now invested in a one-year GIC making 1.8% per year (which earns $900/year). This year she has to take out $10,180 (or $848.33/month). Next year (assuming Betty receives the same rate of return on her GIC), she will have to take out another 20% but she will only have $8290 (or $690/month).

Betty could take out more per year, the 20% is only the minimum amount but that would leave her with even less savings for future years.

When Can I Start taking my CPP & OAS?

When we are asked about when someone should begin taking CPP, our answer is that there is no single best answer, it is completely dependent on your unique situation. This is probably not the answer you would hear from a bunch of 60-to-70 year-old men drinking their coffee at Tim Horton's. If you were to ask these "wise men", you would probably hear this answer: "Haven't you been reading the newspapers? This country is facing financial challenges and the amounts are only going to keep decreasing. Get it while the getting is good—start taking it at age 60!"

Okay, so now we know the Tim Horton's answer, but is that the correct answer? Maybe—maybe not. Again, it all has to do with whether you are still working and if you need that income. We have found that if someone retires at age 60 and has a substantial amount of RRPSs, this may be the perfect time to delay their CPP and draw down on their RRSPs so that they can control the amount of their taxable income later on.

One final important consideration on the matter of when to start taking your portion of the Canada Pension Plan, is your health. If an individual has a serious health condition that significantly lowers his or her odds of a long life, this person might want to take CPP early. Once we pass away, so do our retirement pension cheques, replaced by the survivor benefit cheque, which is a lot less than the average CPP retirement benefit cheque. Thus, it makes much more financial sense to accept CPP benefit payments if the retiree knows he or she will not live far into their 70s.

Now might be the perfect time to explain what the Canada Pension Plan (CPP) and Old Age Security (OAS) are, the impact that they will have on your retirement and why you are receiving or will receive these monthly payments for the rest of your life.

The Canada Pension Plan and Old Age Security are federally managed pensions that provide you with taxable income in retirement. This income is guaranteed, indexed to inflation and arrives in your bank account each month. The starting age for both of these pensions is currently 65. You may not be aware of it, but both you and your employer have been contributing to the Canada Pension Plan with a portion of every paycheque you have ever earned. The benefit will continue to pay out for the rest of your life, and should you pass away before your spouse, they will receive a survivor's pension as well as a small insurance policy to help with final expenses. The Old Age Security benefit is slightly different. Consider OAS a monthly bonus cheque for being Canadian and making it to age 65. You have not contributed to OAS specifically but it does come with certain requirements based on residency, which determines how much of the benefit you get. Once you pass away, though, your OAS cheques stop coming. There is no survivor portion or insurance policy.

Until 2013, Canadians had the option to take an early retirement pension from CPP at age 60 which decreased the monthly pension income by 30% (0.5% a month for 60 months). New legislation has increased the reduction to 31.2% and prescribed a gradual increase to 36.5% by 2016. If you wait until you are 70 to start collecting your CPP, previously you would have received a 30% increase in monthly benefits. If you wait until you are 70 years old, in 2016 you will have increased your monthly benefit by 42%. The government is making it more attractive to defer your CPP payments, and you probably know why. 10 million Baby Boomers are about to start retiring.

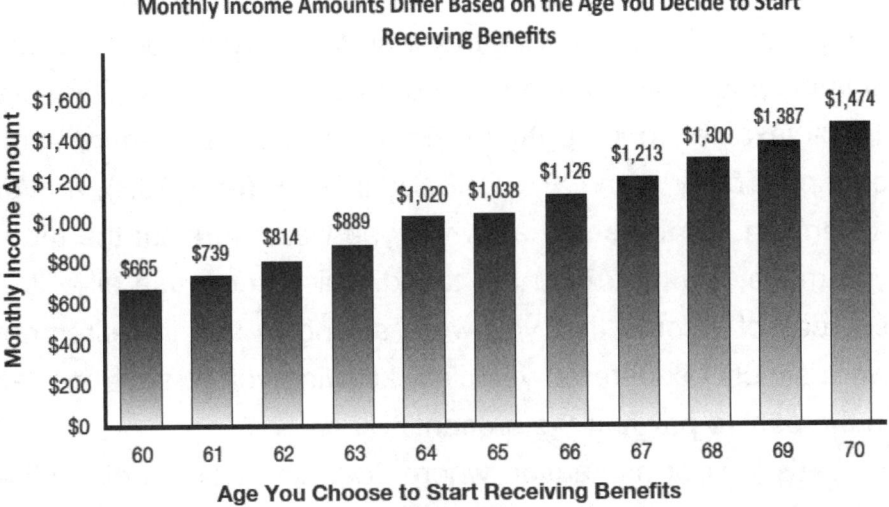

Monthly Income Amounts Differ Based on the Age You Decide to Start Receiving Benefits

This example assumes a benefit of $1,000 at a full retirement age of 66

Source: Service Canada, 2014

There has been a fairly significant change made to OAS recently as well, with the starting age being bumped back to age 67 starting in 2023. This means that if you were born before March 31st of 1958, you're in luck! You can start collecting your OAS at age 65! If you were born after January 31, 1962, you will need to wait until you are 67 to start collecting. Those born between April 1st, 1958, and January 31st, 1962, will have a gradual deferral depending on the exact month and year. That is a lot of money to be missing out on for being born one day later. Talk about a terrible April Fool's joke!

How are CPP and OAS taxed?
And What is this OAS Clawback Nonsense?

Many retirees are surprised when they lose a substantial chunk of their pension, RRIF, and government pension cheques to taxes. That's because all of those sources are considered taxable income—think of them as your new paycheque. They are 100% taxable. To keep things simple, when you're retired and earning money from CPP, OAS, your RRIF (or RRSP), and/or a Pension, it's the same as when you were working; the more you make, the more you are taxed. This is because all of the sources of income that you were saving to use in retirement were simply tax-deferral vehicles, allowing you to save the tax in the past to pay it in the present.

Let's look at a situation where Joe, who worked his entire adult life, retired this year when he turned 65. Joe is one of the lucky few people in Canada who has a defined benefit pension plan from his employer that pays him $2000/month. Joe also has RRSPs and he is planning on taking out $750/ month. He delayed taking his Canada Pension Plan until he was retired, so he'll receive the full amount of $1012.50/ month and he recently started receiving his OAS benefit of $549.89/month. Joe's total monthly taxable income in retirement is just over $4300/month. If Joe's income was over $70,954, his OAS would be subject to what is called the OAS clawback. Since he only made $51,600, he won't be subject to the OAS clawback.

OAS clawback is a real deal, and people can do silly things to make sure that they are able to keep all of their OAS pension and not pay any back to the government. The OAS clawback is the Government of Canada telling you that you do not need their full support in retirement and that they are taking their money back. People view the clawback as punishment for having either planned too well, saved too much, or worked too hard.

It is as uncomfortable as it sounds; ask anyone who has been clawed-back.

Here is what you need to know: if your gross income is more than $70,954 (this number increases each year) on your most recent tax return, then your next year's OAS payments will be decreased by 15% of every dollar you make in excess of the current limit. At the time of writing, the income limit for OAS before clawback is $70,954; this is called the OAS threshold. The amount of income where all of your monthly OAS benefit is clawed-back is $114,640 per individual tax payer.

For example, if you were making $80,000, your repayment would be $80,000 - $70,954 = $9046 x 15% = $1356.90. You will not have to repay this amount; it will be reduced from your future monthly OAS payments as part of recovery tax. Your monthly OAS benefits for the next year would then decrease by $113.08 (which is $1356.90 / 12). We are always asked:

"How can we avoid OAS clawback? It's our money!"

The two additional options for controlling your income to help reduce or avoid the OAS clawback are to invest and redeem from a Tax-Free Savings Account (TFSA) and to purchase a pre-scribed income annuity. Money taken from a TFSA is not considered income, so it will not be included in the calculation used to determine the OAS threshold. Not only does your contribution limit for the TFSA increase each year, but your contribution room actually replenishes to your maximum contribution amount available each year. This means that whatever you take out each year from your TFSA, next year you can add that much back, plus the annual contributions amount. Prescribed annuities spread out the interest earned over the course of your lifetime. By paying the tax this way, your tax bill is significantly lower than what it would be if you were to take a normal annuity.

You will not be able to adjust your income from registered money (your pension, CPP and OAS), you have to take them and you have to pay tax on them. You can adjust your taxable income taken from your RRIF to a certain extent, but generally this is not the best way to control your income because of the regulated minimum withdrawal amounts.

TFSA, Best Thing Since Sliced Bread?

In 2009, the Canadian government introduced a new retirement savings vehicle, the Tax-Free Savings Account (TFSA). Many people are confused by the role that this vehicle is playing and will play in their retirement. This confusion stems from the name; it's quite misleading. It is not so much a tax-free savings account as it is a tax-free investment account. Treating the TFSA like a savings account is like driving a Ferrari only in school zones; it is much more powerful than a savings account.

Starting in 2009, Canadian residents over the age of majority were allowed to contribute $5000 per year into this vehicle. In 2013, the limit was increased to $5500 per year, and contribution room carries forward if unused. The TFSA can hold the same types of investments that are eligible to be held within an RRSP: mutual funds, segregated funds, stocks, bonds, and GICs.

The TFSA differs from an RRSP with respect to the taxation of the investments held within, though. The RRSP provides you with an immediate tax break—whatever amount of money you put in today is deducted from your taxable income for that year. For most people, this means that if they have contributed to their RRSP during the year, they will have overpaid on their taxes and will receive a refund sometime in June. The money within an RRSP grows tax-deferred, meaning there is no tax payable on the growth until it is taken out. When it is taken out, 100% of the withdrawn amount, is then considered taxable income, including all growth. You are saving a few tax dollars today by having the money grow and compound without tax, in order to pay the tax in the future when you finally withdraw that money. For the government, it's like a COD delivery; nothing is paid up front or in transit, but when the money is delivered to you for you to spend, the government takes its cut.

The Tax-Free Savings Account works in the opposite way. You invest into a TFSA with money that you have already paid tax on. This money grows tax-free and when you take it out, any withdrawal is tax-free. Sound pretty good? Well it is. When deciding to invest in either a TFSA or an RRSP there are several things to consider, but we'll focus on the two most glaring issues:

The first thing to consider is that both investment vehicles are designed to perform the same over the long run and provide you with the same amount of net income in retirement. The RRSP is better if you are in a lower-income tax bracket in retirement compared to the tax bracket that you are currently in. For example, if you are making $100,000 now but plan on only taking $50,000 in retirement, then the RRSP is a good option.

The second consideration is a variation of the first consideration. When you receive your tax refund in June after contributing to your RRSP, and you choose to reinvest those proceeds back into your RRSP, the RRSP will be a better option. However, if you're like most Canadians, you're proud of yourself for contributing to your RRSP and you take your refund and go on a vacation or decide to buy something nice for yourself as a reward. In that case, the Tax-Free Savings Account would have been the better long-term option. Long story short, if you are not planning on reinvesting your tax savings into your RRSP, then the TFSA is far and away the better long-term option—you will have the same amount of money in both accounts but the proceeds from the TFSA will pay out tax-free.

Another question that we are frequently asked: "If I am retired, does it make sense to contribute to my TFSA?" Our answer here is: Yes, always. If you have investments that are considered non-registered (which means that they are held outside of your RRSP or RRIF), then you should be maximizing your TFSA every year if possible. Think of it as a conversion. Why would you have your money in an account where you are going to pay tax? Whether the tax is on interest earned, dividends paid, or capital gains when you sell the asset, why pay tax when you don't have to?

How to Repair bear market Damage

One major crisis retirees may face is severe stock market downturns like those we saw in 2008 and 2009. These losses may seem nothing short of debilitating, but there is a way around them. Let's say you are a 75-year-old couple who over the past years have done wonderfully in the market. Your account rose from $250,000, to $500,000, to $600,000. But then, almost overnight, your account dropped back to $500,000. You got on the phone, called your broker, and uttered those famous words: "Get me out."

It now does not matter what anyone advises you—you refuse to leave any more funds in the market. So in your mind, the next logical step is to take the $500,000 to the bank, which kindly offers you a 1% annual return. That is only $5,000 dollars per year in income, which is 100% taxable! You are depressed and disappointed; this money was supposed to help you and your spouse in retirement! You were going to leave some of it to your kids. It looks like the end of the road… but it is not. A rather simple strategy could save your retirement after all.

Here is what we would advise in a market-loss situation such as this one: keep about $100,000 liquid in case of emergency or financial need, then use the other $400,000 to buy a joint lifetime income annuity, which will ensure you and your spouse a paycheque for the rest of either one of your lives. The bonus? The annuity will pay you almost five times what the bank's GIC will. And if one of you lives to age 100, it will even pay you back all the money that you had at the top of the market.

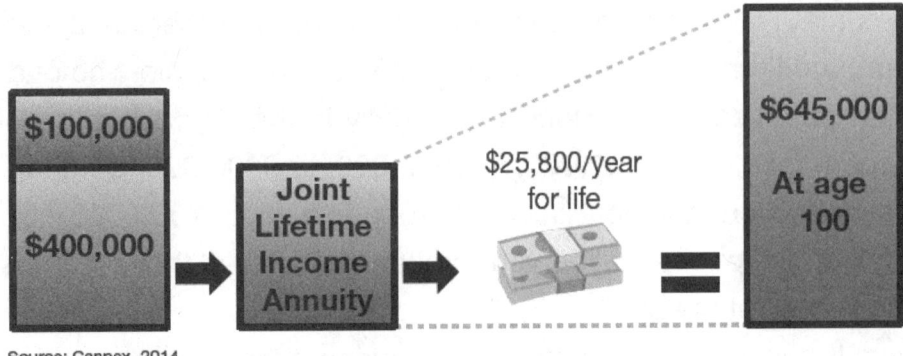

Source: Cannex, 2014

In addition, even if you do not think you will live to 100, you can still guarantee the return of your initial $600,000. This is what you would do: put $500,000 into a joint lifetime income annuity with 25-year certain pay period. You may be pleasantly surprised to see how it works. If you were to invest the $500,000, you will receive yearly income of $28,800. If one of you lives for another 25 years the payout would be $720,000. If both of you were to pass away in 10 years, the remaining payments would continue to be paid out directly to your beneficiaries. While the annual payments are slightly lower than a straight life income annuity, you know that your capital is preserved for your kids or beneficiaries and you have set yourself up with a guaranteed paycheque for the rest of both of your lives.

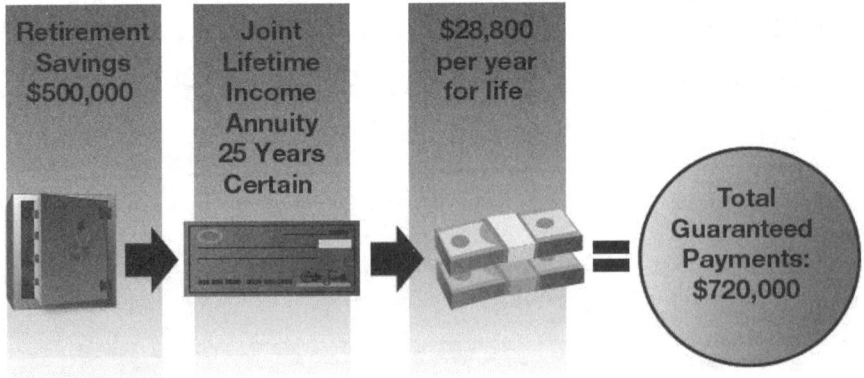

Source: Cannex, 2014

Alternatives to GICs and High-Interest Savings Accounts

Things look brighter now—you have solved your market crisis and left $100,000 in the bank for extra liquidity. But you still cannot help but feel that the bank's interest rates on your $100,000 investment are a little too low, even for such readily-available money. If GICs and savings accounts simply do not cut it for you, there are some other options to consider. An alternative to a bank savings product is a floating-rate bond.

To keep things simple, most bonds are made up of two components: (1) the interest rate paid to the people who own the bond—called the "coupon", and (2) the price that the bond cost to buy in the first place and the amount paid out when the bond matures—called the face value.

How a bond works in its simplest form is: you lend a company like Tim Horton's $1,000 for five years and in return Tim Horton's agrees to pay you 5% interest ($50) every year for five years. At the end of the five years, Tim Horton's will give you your $1,000 back. When you enter into this agreement, the amount is set at $1,000, the term is set at five years, and the interest rate is set at 5%.

Where things get tricky (without going into too much detail) is that when interest rates rise, your 5% bond won't be worth as much as it used to be because Tim Horton's is now selling bonds at 7%.

Enter floating-rate bonds. Despite being relatively new to Canada, the floating-rate bond market in the U.S. is very large in size and very popular with investors.

Think of a floating-rate bond like a variable-rate mortgage. With a variable-rate mortgage, if interest rates go up, so does your monthly cost to borrow that money. The good news for you is that, in this instance, you are not the person borrowing the money—you are the one lending it. So when you own a floating rate bond, the more that interest rates increase the more money you make.

Floating-rate bonds were hurt in the credit crunch of 2008 but mainly because of excessive leveraging and interest rates being continually lowered in an attempt to save the world economy.

Another alternative, especially for those who feel they have too much rotting in liquid reserves, would be to buy a fixed-period immediate income annuity. These are not for life; instead, they generate guaranteed income over a shorter, fixed period of time, such as five or 10 years. When you consider the interest earned and return of premium, investing a chunk of your reserves into one of these annuities could set you up with quite the playcheque, and an absolutely better payout rate than whatever the bank or a credit union offers on GICs. While these are not as liquid as GICs, it is a short-term commitment for a smaller portion of money—a smart way to increase your payout without totally eliminating liquidity and future investment possibilities. The entire amount that went into the fixed-period annuity gets paid out with no principal remaining.

Many among you may feel uneasy about ceding the liquidity of your money to whichever institution manages your RRSP or annuity. Having complete control over one's money, however, does not generate nearly as much income in the end. In general, the retirees who run out of money are exactly those who wanted to be in control and keep their money liquid. Liquidity is not a one-time event - it is a lifetime event. By covering your basic expenses with guaranteed income, you increase your liquidity over your lifetime. By giving up control of some of your money, you gain control over many of the risks in retirement—longevity risk, deflation risk, market risk, withdrawal rate risk, and order of returns risk. These are all risks that you cannot manage when you are trying to control your principal by keeping it in liquid assets. You may very well earn more over time and maintain more liquidity of your other assets, too.

Too many people have a false sense of liquidity—they keep their money in bonds or GICs and use the interest for income. Simultaneously, they count the principal in these accounts as liquid. Yet, if they were to liquidate this money, they would lose their income because there would be no more interest to collect! This common double-counting of assets is a myth that puts many seniors at risk of running out of money.

Enter the Lifetime Income Annuity

	GIC	Lifetime Income Annuity
Initial Investment	$100,000	$100,000
GIC Rate of Return / Annuity Payout Rate	2.50%	6.60%
Total Annual Income	$2,500	$6,600
Tax-Free Income	$0	$4,800
Taxes Owed	$1,075	$775
After-Tax Income	$1,425	$5,825

Source: Cannex, 2014.
** Sample rates, actual rates will vary.

A lifetime income annuity is also a great alternative to a low-yielding GIC. This illustration describes a time when GICs were still paying 2.5%. One couple, looking for a safe return, invested $100,000 in a GIC. Even at 2.5% interest, their annual after-tax income was only $1,425 (a little more than $100/month) on a $100,000 investment. Feeling discouraged by their lack of income, they called their insurance advisor and asked how to improve their income. The advisor said these exact words: "GICs were not made for income." That is what lifetime income annuities were made for. A joint lifetime income annuity would guarantee this family significantly more income for the rest of both lives and still protect their family in case of an early death.

Why are lifetime income annuities able to pay out more than GICs? The answer is that, unlike GICs, there are three components to an annuity paycheque. It is not just interest. It includes principal, interest, and mortality credits. It is really the mortality credits that distinguish lifetime income annuities from other financial products. Mortality credits are a financial reward that increases the longer you live. You have most likely heard from a friend or perhaps even your financial advisor that, because of impending interest rate increases, now is the time to get out of bonds. We bet you have also heard that the stock market is overvalued and due for a correction, and that now is the time to get out of stocks. So if you shouldn't be investing in bonds because their value is going to go down, and you shouldn't be investing in stocks because they are overvalued, and GICs barely give you anything... where do you put your money so you can make more money? Good news!

There are so many different types of annuities available, with options for almost any circumstance.

Leaving a Legacy: How Never to be Forgotten

Why do grandparents and grandchildren get along so well? They have a common enemy—or so the old joke goes. But all kidding aside, most grandparents do want to leave some sort of legacy to their grandchildren. How about a guaranteed lifetime payment for both you and your grandchildren?

If we were asked to set up a retirement plan for a 75-year-old client and he said, "I've got this beautiful 18-year-old granddaughter. I want to do something special for her. Now, some people say I should buy life insurance, but others say I shouldn't. Some people say I should put it in a Registered Education Savings Plan, some others say I shouldn't. Do you have any ideas?"

We would tell him: "Yes, we've got some ideas. But before we give you our ideas, we've got to prove a point." And he would be handed a piece of paper. On this piece of paper, there are four lines on the top and eight lines on the bottom. "On these top four lines, do us a favour—jot down the first and last names of your four grandparents—grandma and grandpa on your mom's side, grandma and grandpa on your dad's side. Their first and last names. Everybody can do it."

On average, only about half of everyone reading this book can list the first and last names of all four of their grandparents. Isn't that amazing? Then we asked him, "On these eight lines, do me a favour—jot down the first and last names of your eight great-grandparents. Go ahead; it should just take a minute. We'll wait." Needless to say, none of us has ever been on an appointment where somebody could remember the first and last names of their eight great-grandparents.

"You know what's so interesting about that? John D. Rockefeller's great-great-great-grandkids all remember his first and last name. How could John D. Rockefeller's great-great-great-grandkids remember him, while you don't even remember your own grandma and grandpa? Well, it's because every year they get a cheque from John D. Rockefeller." John D. Rockefeller always said to leave something behind, and that he most definitely did.

Our recommendation was to set up a joint lifetime annuity between the grandpa and his 18-year-old granddaughter. We told him: "To make this even more special, we will ask the insurance company to make the payment each year on your granddaughter's birthday. For the rest of your life, every time she has a birthday, you're going to get a cheque from the insurance company and you can use that to put in a life insurance policy. You can put it towards her university tuition. You could buy her a car. If she decides to not attend university, you can spend it on yourself. Regardless, for the rest of your life, every time she has a birthday, you're going to get a cheque from the insurance company. But, starting from the day you die, that beautiful granddaughter is going to get a present from her favourite grandpa every birthday for the rest of her life. She's never going to forget you. She's going to remember you on line number one, just like John D. Rockefeller's descendants. And on the day that your grand-daughter dies, your great-granddaughter is going to get half of all the money you ever put in this account. She'll get it income tax-free. She's going to remember you right there on line number one as well."

Here is how it works in practice: You have a generous grandpa. He possesses $100,000 of lazy money. He buys a joint life lifetime income annuity and a paid up life insurance contract (with a separate insurance policy with a death benefit of $50,000 on his granddaughter's life). The joint annuitant is his 18-year-old granddaughter. For the rest of his life, he gets $3,165 every year that she has a birthday (again, these payout rates can change, so check with your financial advisor for an updated quote). When grandpa dies, she continues to get a birthday present of $3,165 every birthday for the rest of her life. Let me pause right there. If you had a grandparent who gave you $3,165 every birthday for your entire life, would you remember him or her? Probably. And on the day that the granddaughter dies, the great-granddaughter will receive half of the original deposit: $50,000 income, tax-free. If you had a great-grandma or great-grandpa who left you $50,000 tax-free, don't you think that might separate them from the pack a little bit?

You may be wondering, "What about inflation?" With an annuity, you can also purchase an inflation-protection rider. You can add an inflation factor on it so that the annuity payout increases each year with inflation. Her 18 year old birthday present goes down to $1,100, but every year that goes up by 5%. When she is 30, it is $1,850. When she is 50, it is $3,500.00. When she is 65, it is $5,250. Now if the granddaughter lives to be 100, which by the way is a distinct possibility, she will get yearly payments of $15,000 plus the $50,000 death benefit, a total payout on that original $100,000 investment of $500,000. Where else can a grandpa take $100,000, be guaranteed that two generations of his family will never forget his name, and out of that $100,000, potentially transfer $500,000? That grandparent could be you!

Annuity with Inflation Protection

Granddaughter's Age	Annual Birthday Present
18	$1,300
30	$1,825
50	$3,500
65	$5,250
Death Benefit	$50,000

Source: Cannex, 2014
* Note: These are sample payment rates, actual rates will vary.

Customized Solutions to Everyday Retirement Problems

 Key Points from Chapter 5

1. You can generate a hassle-free guaranteed income for life by using a lifetime income annuity to satisfy your required minimum withdrawals from your RRIF. If you are married, consider using a joint life annuity with cash refund option. Remember, you don't owe your kids a nickel of your RRSP or RRIF—you saved that for your retirement!

2. With CPP and OAS, do what is right for your particular situation and don't be afraid to ask your financial advisor for their opinion as well, they are asked this all the time.

3. Consider an annuity on your non-registered money to help keep your taxable income to a minimum, so your OAS isn't clawed back.

4. Everyone should consider converting his or her non-registered investments into a Tax-Free Savings Account up to the maximum amount allowable each year.

5. People in their seventies who have lost money in the market, should consider using a joint life annuity with a life cash refund to help get back much or all of what was lost.

6. GICs weren't made for income—that is what a lifetime income annuity was made for!

7. You can have your descendants remember your name, just like John D. Rockefeller. Use a joint lifetime income annuity with a paid up life insurance policy to create a multi-generational payout system.

Chapter 6

Annuities: Insure Your Investments

We are always amazed at the reactions we receive from people when we use the word "annuity". Some people absolutely love annuities. Some people hate annuities. Some think they know exactly what an annuity is because their grandmother receives $435 every month from a major Canadian insurance company. Others are wary of annuities because they do not understand them.

This chapter will try to clear up any misconceptions you might have about annuities. The truth is that any product on its own is neither good nor bad. Considering what the product does, what the product is, and how the product is used will help you understand annuities more clearly and decide if one would make sense for you. Annuities are actually risk management tools. You can transfer many of the retirement risks we have discussed to an insurance company. Market risk, longevity risk, inflation risk, deflation risk, order of returns risk, and withdrawal rate risk can all be transferred to an insurance company. You can, in fact, insure your investments. Annuities can do things that no other product in the world can do. But if that is true, why do so many people hate annuities? It is not that annuities are bad, but rather that there are bad annuities. Unfortunately, too many people have had unfavourable experiences with annuities or know someone who has. This has led some people to simply declare that all annuities are bad. That is simply not true.

In the meantime, it is necessary to understand annuities in general. Annuities are purchased through insurance companies. There are hundreds of annuities in the marketplace today, but based on their payout strategies, all of these annuities can be separated into two broad categories: immediate annuities and deferred annuities. That's it. There are no other choices. So let's take a look at both.

Immediate Annuities

An immediate annuity works when a lump sum is paid to an insurance company. Normally, payments begin immediately or within 12 months. We say "normally" because as we write this book, there are a couple of companies who allow you to now defer that income up to 15 years! An immediate annuity's primary purpose is to provide guaranteed income. This income can either be guaranteed for a period of time (fixed-period annuities) or for your entire life (lifetime income annuities).

Fixed-Period Annuities

A fixed-period annuity is a type of immediate annuity that pays a guaranteed income for a fixed period of time (for example, five, 10, or 20 years). This annuity provides a certain amount of income for a specified period of time. It can be used in real estate transactions or to pay annual obligations like life insurance premiums over a period of time. Once that time is over, the payments stop and there is no more money in the annuity. It has completely paid out. Each paycheque from a fixed period annuity contains both principal and interest. No mortality credits are paid in a fixed period annuity.

Fixed-period annuities are more popular when interest rates are high, as they were in the 1970s and 1980s. Recently, however, fixed-period annuities have been less attractive because of today's low interest rate environment. Fixed-period annuities have no fees or charges—they are a spread product, which means the insurance company has to make more money than what they are paying you in order to make a profit. Any "loads" are part of the pricing of the product. You will know exactly how much you will receive for the stated period of time and premium you give them.

Lifetime Income Annuities

The second type of immediate annuity is a lifetime income annuity. Some people know it as a single premium immediate annuity (SPIA). This book is focused on this type of annuity because you simply cannot retire properly without one. As we discussed earlier, a lifetime income annuity is a guaranteed paycheque for life.

Both registered (RRSP or RRIF) and non-registered money can be used in these annuities. Some popular examples of life income annuities are OAS, CPP and company-defined benefit pension plans. Most Canadians will receive at least one or two of these and perhaps don't realize that they have a life income annuity.

Lifetime income annuities have many different options which make them flexible and allow you to make significant decisions based on what is best for you and your beneficiaries. The income can be based on one life or two lives. The two lives can be any two people—husband and wife, father and son, even two golfing buddies. This product also works well with same-sex couples. A joint lifetime income annuity between husband and wife, for example, means that if you pass away and your spouse remains alive, payments will continue for the remainder of your spouse's life. Different guarantee options are available: you can choose no guarantee beyond your life, or you can have your initial premium (minus the payments received) guaranteed to your beneficiaries, which would be paid to them in a cash refund, a lump sum, or installment payments. You can also have life with period certain guaranteed. This option will pay you for the rest of your life, but if you die prematurely, it will continue the payments for a period of time.

If all of this seems confusing, it really isn't. When you get an illustration from your financial or insurance professional, all of these options will be listed and the payout rate will be different for each one. So which choice is best? That is totally up to you. Neither the insurance company nor your financial or insurance professional has a financial incentive to push one option over the other. This decision depends on what is most important to you and your family, your health, and your best guess at your life expectancy. Sometimes people take out more than one annuity with different guarantees to maximize potential benefits.

Only about 8% of all lifetime income annuities take the life only option (according to a Major Life Insurance Company's experience). So 92% of all lifetime income annuity buyers want a guarantee in case of their premature death. When we really started getting involved with lifetime income annuities, we were big fans of life with cash refund. It certainly is the easiest to explain and understand. If you give the insurance company $100,000 and they guarantee to pay you $10,000 per year, and you die after two years, your family gets the remaining $80,000. On the other hand, if you live for 20 years, the insurance company has to pay you a total of $200,000. That is a very simple proposition, and simple is usually best.

However, the more we have studied these products and the research surrounding them, the more we are believers in life-only or joint life-only. This is where you maximize the benefits of mortality credits. In fact, when it comes time for me (Rob) to buy my lifetime income annuities, my plan is to buy joint life payouts for my wife and I. We will leave our kids other assets. In fact, by using life only, the research shows you will probably be able to leave your children more money. So while everyone buys guarantees just in case they die early, at least half of these people—probably closer to 65%—would be better off taking a life-only contract.

WITHDRAWAL RIGHTS

Many people believe that lifetime income annuities are illiquid investments, meaning that the principal is untouchable outside of scheduled payments. For example, you cannot go to the Canada Pension Plan Administration and ask for a $50,000 withdrawal from your future CPP benefits. However, with your lifetime income annuity, some life insurance companies will allow you to ask for a withdrawal of a lump sum. Each company handles withdrawals differently, so you will want to ask for specifics.

Generally, the insurance company would take the amount of guaranteed payments you have remaining and apply a calcu-lation to determine what amount of withdrawal is possible. So, a number of lifetime income annuities offer more flexibility than most people think.

PAYMENT OPTIONS

Insurance companies are becoming very helpful in addressing client objections to lifetime income annuities. We just discussed how many have incorporated guarantees and withdrawal priv-ileges into their annuities. Other features are continually being incorporated into annuity plans from many companies.

How about flexibility in payment amounts? Some people would like to have larger cheques initially while waiting for Can-ada Pension, Old Age Security or other pension income to start, then have lower annuity cheques once these other sources of income begin. Others would rather have lower paycheques from their annuity now, while a business or real estate sale is providing them income, but want larger cheques in the future when these payments stop. These options offer tremendous flexibility as your needs change.

A new option provides flexibility in payment timing. There are a couple of companies who now allow you to defer taking income from an annuity for one, two, five, 10, or up to 15 years in exchange for a higher payout rate. This type of annuity is called a deferred income annuity, although it falls under the immediate annuity umbrella. The payout rates of these products are very compelling. For example, someone in their mid-50s who wants income at age 65 could have guaranteed payout rates of 7.5%. Someone age 65 who wants to start income at age 80 as a form of "longevity insurance" could very well receive a guaranteed payout rate near 15%!

INFLATION PROTECTION

Many lifetime income annuities offer inflation protection. You can have your paycheque go up by 1%, 2%, or even up to 5% per year. Naturally, your initial paycheque will be lower or you will have to put more money in to keep payment amounts constant over time. Less than 4% of all lifetime income annuities sold have inflation protection on them. Why so low? Perhaps because the initial paycheque amount drops significantly once inflation protection is added. Also, as people age into their 80s and 90s, they tend to spend less and less each year, which can serve as a form of unofficial inflation protection. A big exception here would be all of the seniors who did not purchase long-term care insurance. Many of those people will likely end up spending most or all of their money on end-of-life care.

A strategy that offers inflation protection with maximum flexibility is to ladder your lifetime income annuity purchases. That just means you do not have to spend all of your money on a lifetime income annuity. You can buy one that covers your basic expenses and invest the rest of your money with inflation in mind. Stocks and commodities, for example, are sensitive to inflation. If inflation goes up, these investments should rise as well. You can take some of those profits to buy another lifetime income annuity later on to give your income inflation protection as well. Repeat as necessary throughout your retirement. This keeps more of your money liquid, while still protecting you from an inflationary environment.

FEES AND TAXES

Just like a fixed-period annuity, a lifetime income annuity is a spread product and normally has no annual fees and charges. You will know exactly how much per month you will receive, based on the amount you give the insurance company. One huge benefit of the lifetime income annuity is the taxation of the payments. For non-registered money (outside of an RRSP or RRIF), only a portion of the monthly payment is taxable. Remember, each paycheque consists of principal, interest, and mortality credits. The principal is not taxable. For example, $12,000 of annual income from a lifetime income annuity may only result in $3,000-$4,000 of taxable income! This amount will be shown on the illustration you receive from your financial advisor. With non-registered funds you can choose between a prescribed annuity (where the amount of taxable income reportable each year is a fixed and level amount so you always know what your net after tax paycheque will be) or a non-prescribed annuity where the tax calculation varies and is typically higher taxable amount in the earlier years to reflect the higher proportion of interest early on but lower or eliminated in later years. When registered money is used to buy an annuity all payments are fully taxable.

Deferred Annuities

The deferred annuity is a type of annuity used for saving and investing. In contrast to the immediate annuity, deferred annuities do not begin payments right away, but rather allow your money to grow over time. An advantage of a deferred annuity is that it can be turned into income at any time. There are two ways to do this. First, you can annuitize the contract. This annuitization literally turns a deferred annuity into a lifetime income annuity. Annuitization is the process of collecting income from your annuity, so annuitization in a deferred annuity would not happen until payments started. Many annuities also offer the option to turn income on and off. You can determine what amount you want per month. This amount can be changed or stopped at any time. For example, if you begin collecting payments and then sell your house, you can put payments on hold and live off the lump sum from the house sale. This way the principal in your annuity continues to collect interest and grow. Just make sure that when you make withdrawals, they do not violate the withdrawal terms of your annuity and subject you to unnecessary surrender charges and/or tax penalties.

If you annuitize the contract, understand that payout rates vary, so you would want to compare the annuitization payout rate offered by the deferred annuity versus the payout rate from a new lifetime income annuity when you are ready to start collecting your paycheque. Some companies use a higher rate for their new lifetime income annuities than the annuitization rate from their deferred annuities.

Why would these differences exist? Possibly because many people have no idea how these contracts work, and it is easier to just annuitize an existing contract than to shop around for higher payout rates. Deferred annuities also offer guarantees which are discussed below that are not offered by other products.

Fixed Deferred Annuities

Like immediate annuities, there are two types of deferred annuities—fixed and variable. A fixed deferred annuity is the insurance company's version of a Guaranteed Investment Certificate or GIC (although fixed annuities are insured through Assuris, not CDIC). Every day, the value of a fixed deferred annuity goes up. Sometimes, fixed deferred annuities pay a higher rate of interest than GICs! If you are looking for a fixed annuity, here is some advice that will keep you out of trouble. First, look for the highest rated insurance companies. Then, compare the interest rates offered from these highly-rated carriers. Finally, look for a money-back guarantee at any time just in case you change your mind or have some type of emergency. If you follow those simple rules, you will never be burned by a fixed deferred annuity.

Just like fixed immediate annuities, fixed deferred annuities are spread products, so there are normally no annual fees. You will get exactly the interest rate that they declare. Remember, however, this is an annual interest rate. There is no daily or weekly compounding of interest. It is compounded annually. In addition, fixed deferred annuities may have surrender charges (similar to an early withdrawal penalty).

Some fixed annuities are single premium while others are flexible premium. Flexible premium simply means you can add money to the contract—normally at any time, subject to a minimum deposit amount. Check the contract to see how yours works.

Guaranteed minimum Withdrawal Benefit (GMWB)

In 2006 the first Guaranteed Minimum Withdrawal Benefit (GMWB) contract was introduced in Canada. The idea had been popular in the U.S. for a few years and many thought that it would catch on in Canada given the similar Baby Boomer demographic.

Between 2006 and 2012 we experienced extreme market volatility and historically low interest rates. Both of these factors dramatically affect the pricing and profitability of the GMWB from the insurance companies perspective. Over that same period, a number of insurance companies introduced, modified and (some) even withdrew completely from the GMWB market. At the time of writing there are still a couple of companies that offer a version of the GMWB.

A GMWB contract guarantees that no matter what the market does, the client will be guaranteed a minimum income for life once they start taking income (usually at 65 or later although some contracts allow the income to start as early as age 55). This takes market risk off the table as well as longevity risk. So, if the market goes up, your account value will go up and you can draw income off of the investment based on the higher of the market value or the guaranteed minimum, whichever is greater.

However, if the market goes down, you are guaranteed an income based on the original amount invested plus any bonuses credited. These step-up or bonus guarantees of 3% to 7% allow you to calculate a minimum income guarantee at the future desired date. An important thing to remember in a GMWB contract is that you must annuitize the contract (start taking income) to receive that guarantee.

This whole book has been about the importance of annuitizing assets in retirement, so this would be a great product, right? Not necessarily. To give this guarantee, the insurance company cannot give you the same annuitization (payout) rates as a fixed lifetime income annuity. Most of these contracts reduce the rate by an amount similar to subtracting 10 years from your age at the time of purchase. So, the annuitization rate with a GMWB for a 70-year-old would be about 5% or 5.5% lifetime income which is similar to the payout of a 60-year-old buying a lifetime income annuity.

This 70-year-old could get a better rate of return than 7%, but it is still a better guarantee than you would have in a mutual fund or individual stocks and bonds.

Most of these contracts also guarantee a minimum bonus factor of 3%-7%. Many people buying these contracts believe that their principal is guaranteed to grow by a certain percentage each year. If the market goes up, they get the upside of the market. But if the market falls, they think their cash value will go up by 5%. That is not true. These contracts have two values—the cash value (or market value) and the benefit base value. The cash value goes up and down with the market, so guaranteed growth does not apply to this value. The benefit base, however, is guaranteed to grow by a minimum rate. There may also be a reset provision to the benefit base if the market goes up by more than the annual guarantee.

Investors need to know that the benefit base is not the principal—the market value is. You cannot take all of that benefit base money out. If you choose to cash in the plan you would get the market value, minus any fees or penalties. When you die, your family would receive the greater of the market value or the death benefit guarantee. The benefit base is simply used to calculate your withdrawal benefit (normally 3% to 7% of the benefit base). While these GMWB contracts will guarantee income for your retirement, they are also a guarantee that can help give you confidence to stay in the market during turbulent times because of the downside protection. If the market does well, you will probably be much better off transferring into a lifetime income annuity and receiving a higher income after any surrender period on the segregated fund has expired.

The main problem with this type of variable annuity is that the fees can get very high—3% or more in some cases. Your principal could very well run out in this type of annuity. However, your income is guaranteed for life as long as you do not violate any other provisions of the contract. Just be careful to clearly understand what you are buying.

Fees - By the Numbers

There are four simple questions you should ask your financial professional or advisor before ever investing a penny into anything.

1. Is there a front end load?
Front end loads are charges or commissions assessed at the time of investment; the fee is deducted from your investment amount, thereby lowering the total principal. Annuities typically have no front load.

2. Is there any type of policy fee or annual maintenance fee?
Most fixed annuities will not have these, although some will charge a fee for smaller accounts. Variable annuities (segregated funds) may charge a fee for smaller accounts and will charge a fee for guaranteed living benefits and the reset death benefit rider.

3. Are there any hidden charges?
Not with fixed or lifetime income annuities. However, in variable annuities you will have a mortality and expense charge (which covers the death benefit and some of the other features) of anywhere from about 1% to 1.85% annually. Additionally, there is an annual fund management fee on these accounts; such fees range from .4% to over 2%, but the average is 1%.

4. Are there any surrender charges and what are they?

Surrender charges are fees assessed if you withdraw funds from your account before an agreed-upon date; the "surrender period" must pass before you can withdraw without this charge. These fees will normally range from 0% to 6% depending on how long you have held the annuity at withdrawal. Surrender periods are usually two to seven years, at which time the charges will be eliminated, but some annuities can have much longer surrender periods. We would avoid annuities with high surrender fees or long surrender periods. On the bright side, you can buy annuities with no surrender charge at all. As you would expect, they do not offer the same level of features or guarantees.

Many people do not realize that segregated funds can technically be considered annuities. We have already discussed segregated funds in detail but because they are annuities, we felt that they should be re-introduced. There are countless cases of people who invested in the stock market and lost entire fortunes. As far as we know, no one has ever lost their entire fortune investing in segregated funds; that is because segregated funds offer guarantees that protect your principal. Segregated funds can protect your assets over the long term so you can invest confidently. This confidence comes from knowing that segregated funds offer the potential growth of the stock market with reduced exposure to risk through their guarantees.

Dealing with Market Risk

Now that we have covered the mechanics and features of annuities, it is important to consider how they can help you limit market risk during turbulent times. Dealing with market volatility and its impact on your retirement assets has been extremely difficult given the wild market gyrations of years past. In general, there are three things a good financial advisor can do to help you tolerate market risk: one, they can help you manage market risk; two, they can help you put a floor under market risk; and three, they can help you eliminate market risk.

1. Managing Market Risk

First of all, when it comes to managing risk, we like to use the example of the 1987 stock market crash, one of the worst in the history of the U.S. stock market. This crash happened long enough ago that we can look at it now with a great deal of perspective. Looking at the chart below, you can see that the market crashed 23% in one day. For those of us who remember that day, the level of panic was something we had never seen before.

While rumors of stockbrokers jumping out of windows to commit suicide were proven to be false, there was still a widespread panic across the country that many of us had never experienced. The average investor had no idea what to do, and many sold just in time to lock in their losses (as the market soon regained its footing and continued to climb for decades).

By putting risk into perspective, we can learn from the past and apply our knowledge to the future. As Warren Buffet said, "Buy when others are fearful, and be fearful when others are buying." The chart on the next page shows the exact same 1987 stock market crash, but now in the framework of decades of stock market performance. Notice how (over the long term) those days of panic are merely blips amid the constant general upward climb of the market.

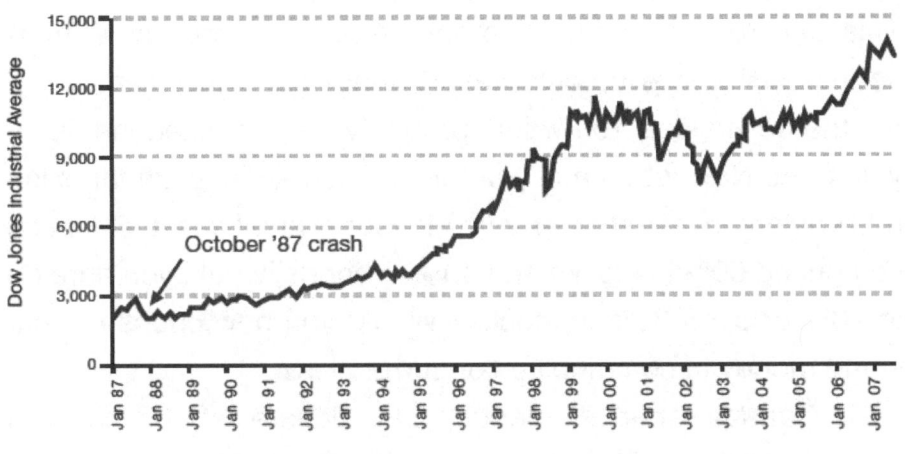

The Market in October 1987 through 2007

Source: TomHegna.com and *The Wall Street Journal*

You will not need to panic about market volatility if you understand the key tenets to successful investing: invest for the long term, diversify your portfolio, and utilize proper asset allocation with regular rebalancing. Because of the lost decade of the 2000s in the stock market, many people say these tenets are dead, or that you have to day trade in order to make money. When it comes to day trading, here is our advice: if you want to make a small fortune in day trading, start with a large fortune. No one knows what the market is going to do, or when. No one. It is important to keep that in perspective.

2. Putting a Floor Under Market Risk

This leads us into our second point—putting a floor under market risk. What if you could have the upside of the market, but not the downside? You would probably be interested in this investment. Now let us ask you this: if such an investment existed, would you invest differently? If your normal asset allocation comprised 60% in stocks and 40% in bonds, would you dare go to 70% or even 80% in stocks? Would you now choose to put some money in commodities or currencies?

In Canada, an investment like this does exist. It is called a segregated fund. This investment allows you to choose your stock and/or bond funds, invest in the market, and capture the full upside of the market, but you are guaranteed not to lose a penny over a certain period of time—normally 10 years. These products also come with a guaranteed death benefit that protects your family from market losses upon your death. For example, suppose you invested $100,000 in a segregated fund with a 100% maturity guarantee. You would be guaranteed to get your original $100,000 back at the end of the 10-year period even if your investments were worth less than that due to market losses. If you pass away during the 10-year period, the death benefit would provide your beneficiaries with, at minimum, the amount of your initial investment. While you have to pay a fee for these risk management provisions up front, it will insure that your investment never falls below what you started with.

Both of these guarantees can typically be stepped-up or re-set on each policy anniversary up to a certain age. The step-up allows you to lock in gains and therefore will increase your guaranteed death benefit and maturity benefit. For example, suppose you invested $100,000 with an annual step-up. If after a year the value of your investment increased to $125,000, you could lock in the $125,000 as the new value of your guaranteed maturity benefit. This step-up means that you will be guaran-teed at least the $125,000 ten years from your step-up date regardless of future market performance.

In Tom's seminars, he has challenged his audiences to show him any place in the world where he can invest his money that will give him, after fees, more upside with lower downside. A pretty simple challenge. And yet, after nearly 3,000 seminars, he has yet to be presented an alternative to his variable annuity that will satisfy those simple requirements.

While critics seem to focus on the fees, which can be higher than no-load mutual funds, they always overlook the value of the product for many investors. We have been on thousands of appointments, and in nearly all of them, the client wanted to make as much as they could on their investment. If they can make 10%, 20%, 30%, or even 50%, they will take as much as the market will give them. We have never found anyone who wanted to put a cap on the upside of their investments. At the same time, however, these same people do not want to lose what they already have.

As we discussed, segregated funds with guaranteed minimum withdrawal benefits are all the rage. These products also put a floor on risk but in a slightly different manner. They guarantee a minimum withdrawal amount that can be used for income in retirement. However, they do not guarantee the cash value. Also, many advisors think these are income-producing vehicles. While they can be, the truly sharp financial professional recognizes that these are, in fact, sub-optimal income producers. When income is actually needed, there are many better options (the lifetime income annuity certainly comes to mind). Their real value is giving the client some amount of guarantee on their investment, which gives them the confidence to stay in the market during turbulent times. Remember, the primary purpose of a segregated fund is growth—not income.

3. Eliminating Market Risk

The third option for market risk is to simply eliminate it. In our combined 60+ years in the insurance and investment business, we have met plenty of people who have just had it with risk and the stock market. No matter how convincing we are, we would never be able to convince them to rejoin the market. We are sure you know people just like that, or perhaps you are one yourself. It's okay—there are many, many wealthy people who do not believe in taking risks with their savings and investments. The fact is that you do not have to take risks with your investments to have a successful retirement.

Fixed deferred annuities, as we discussed earlier, are products that guarantee both the principal and interest. You invest money in the annuity and agree not to withdraw it for a certain period of time. Not surprisingly, fixed deferred annuities tend to pay a higher rate of interest than GICs.

Other people focus on the CDIC insurance that protects GIC buyers. Some buyers are even so diligent as to spread their GICs over many banks. We always wonder if these people have actually researched CDIC insurance. We have. If you go to the CDIC website (www.cdic.ca), you can read up on the history of CDIC insurance.

Seriously, a far better option would be to look at the fixed deferred annuities offered by top-rated insurance companies. Of course, another great way to eliminate market risk is to buy a lifetime income annuity. As we have talked about (and will continue to talk about), a lifetime income annuity is a guaranteed paycheque for life—a lifetime of paycheques with an incredibly attractive payout rate and no market risk. This is truly a product meant to help you have a happy and successful retirement. So there you have it—if you are going to be in the market, manage your risk or put a floor under it. Keep in mind, though, that you do not have to be in the the market if you feel it is just not right for you.

ANNUITY TIMELINE - THEY ARE OLDER THAN YOU THINK

AD 225

A Roman judge named Ulpianus produced the first known mortality table for "annua," which were lifetime stipends made once a year in exchange for a lump-sum payment

1600s

"Tontines" became popular with European governments to pay for wars and public works projects. A tontine gave each participant income for life, with the payment increasing to the survivors as other participants passed away. Payments ceased upon the death of all the participants.

1700s

British Parliament authorized annuity sales. Annuities became popular among European "high society," as a form of prevention from a fall from grace, unavailable in other, more risky investments.

1905

Andrew Carnegie established the Teacher's Pension Fund. This eventually became TIAA—Teachers Insurance and Annuity Association—in 1918 to provide annuities to educators.

1908

Canadian Government Annuities Act was passed. Its purpose was to encourage Canadians to prepare financially for their retirement

1927

Old Age Pensions Act (OAP) was passed by Canadian Government to provide means-tested pension for men and women 70 years of age and older.

1930s

During the Great Depression, investors looked to annuities and life insurance as safe havens from financial ruin.

1951

Old Age Security Act (OAS) replaced OAP. It introduced a universal flat-rate pension for people 70 and older with residency requirements.

1965

Prime Minister Lester B. Pearson first established the Canadian Pension Plan (CPP).

2011

Individual annuity sales in Canada top $1.57 billion.

Annuities: Insure Your Investments

 Key Points from Chapter 6

1. Annuities are simply a RISK MANAGEMENT TOOL.

2. Annuities are not bad but there ARE "bad" annuities.

3. There are only two types of annuities—immediate or deferred.

4. Immediate annuities provide guaranteed income.

5. Deferred annuities provide growth with additional benefits and guarantees. There are two types of deferred annuities—fixed and variable.

6. Variable annuities or segregated funds offer many features and benefits that can literally allow you to "insure" your investments and have some peace of mind in turbulent times.

7. When it comes to market risk—manage it, put a floor under it, or eliminate it!

Chapter 7

Life Insurance: The Miracle Money Machine

In past chapters, we have discussed how changing trends in the economy, public policy, and overall life expectancy have completely altered the rules of the retirement game. By this point, though, hopefully we have convinced you that there are real ways that you can still have the retirement of your dreams. In fact, one of the reasons you are still reading this book is that we have promised to prove to you that you can have a guaranteed stream of income for the rest of your life— something you have just learned about with annuities.

But in today's changed world, what other options do you have to ensure that your family is provided for, your money is safe, your portfolio is optimized, and your money flow does not screech to a halt when your career finally does? How can you not only plan successfully for unforeseen expenses, but for the ultimate foreseen expense? Here, life insurance makes its grand entrance. This chapter is all about how and why you should greet it with open arms and welcome it into your retirement plan.

The Great Comeback

Let us ask you a question. What if you had a money machine in your garage that delivered $10,000 every month. Would you put insurance on it? We bet you would. In fact, we would put a video camera on it and hook it up to my smart phone with a beeper so we could see if anyone messed with my money machine! Well, guess what, YOU are that machine! Every month you bring home income. You need to make sure that income arrives every month for your family, even if you don't come home someday!

While it might strike you as morbid at first, planning your retirement with the inevitable in mind can enable you to retire more securely, eliminate anxiety about providing for your family, and give you rewarding cash returns in the long run. Having a plan for the long-term must be taken very seriously, and no retirement is complete without one. But having a plan in the form of "some money put away in the bank for a retirement home" is just not good enough. We see your plan and raise you cash value, tax benefits, estate and tax-free income creation, and the priceless feeling of knowing your family will be financially secure after you are gone.

Your grandparents relied on it to carry them through the Great Depression, as the life insurance industry prevailed without the serious problems experienced in other sectors of the economy. However, for most of you, the idea of life insurance might seem surprising—especially the concept of permanent life insurance. For the past 20 years, term life insurance has lit up the radar screen, while permanent life insurance has faded into the background. Why? The '80s and '90s saw a thriving stock market, more guaranteed pensions, and indexed government pension plans, which made investing in a life insurance policy seem weak and ultra-risk-averse at a time when investing in the market promised to yield huge earnings—and in many cases, it did. But today, with the stock market as unstable as it is, defined benefit pensions disappearing like the dinosaurs, CPP and OAS in the throes of upheaval and change, that old permanent life policy people scoffed at for years suddenly looks like the better deal for those headed into retirement. And that's because it is.

Some high-profile financial commentators have advised millions to skip permanent life insurance policies. Their advice was to "buy term and invest the difference." Unfortunately, an entire generation bought into that opinion. But rather than buying term and investing the difference, they bought term and spent the difference. Or, even worse, bought term and lost the difference! Now an entire generation of Canadians is approaching retirement without any permanent life insurance. They were told that their house would be paid off (it isn't), that they would have a pension (they don't), that their kids would be on their own (they're not), and that there would be no need for any life insurance (but there is). Where are those so-called experts now?

The Miracle of Life Insurance

The late Ben Feldman, one of the greatest life insurance advisors in history, often referred to life insurance as a miracle. Make no mistake about it: life insurance truly is a miracle in that it delivers exactly the right amount of money at exactly the right time. Think about it. What other financial instrument can guarantee a specific amount of dollars exactly when it is needed?

Feldman referred to life insurance as simply a drop of ink, a piece of paper, and a promise. Life insurance promises to:

Take care of your family if you die too soon. They can live in the same home, attend the same schools, go to college, and maintain the same lifestyle they are accustomed to, even though you are not there to take care of them.

Take care of you if you live too long—the cash value of the policy can be withdrawn tax-free or turned into a lifetime income annuity.

Function as a self-completing plan. Even if you are disabled, a waiver of premiums can guarantee that your plan will be completed even if you are unable to make further premiums.

Provide immediate cash in the case of a terminal illness. Clients have used this cash to re-

ceive extraordinary medical treatment, which
can delay death for many years. Others use it
to get their affairs in order prior to death.

Feldman had a way of simplifying the concepts surrounding
life insurance. Here are some of our favourite Feldman quotes
on this subject:

"Life insurance is time. The time that man
might not have. If he needs time, he needs life
insurance."

"The basic purpose of life insurance is to create
cash...nothing more and nothing less. Everything else confuses and complicates."

"Life insurance is the only tool that takes pennies and guarantees dollars."

Let us give you a perspective on life insurance that you may
never have considered. Remember when we discussed the importance of mortality credits when using a lifetime income annuity in retirement? Life insurance uses those same mortality
credits! How else could a 20-year-old write a cheque for $25
to an insurance company, leave the appointment, step in front
of a speeding bus, and then have their family receive a cheque
for $1 million from that insurance company? See, the insurance
company knows that not many 20-year-olds are going to die, so
a young person can take advantage of mortality credits through

the miracle of life insurance. Some people call this leverage—and it is—but it is a very specific form of leverage that is based in mortality credits. Those same mortality credits allow an 85-year-old widow to write the insurance company a small cheque and receive large monthly payments for the rest of her life. Here is the deal: the risk to an insurance company when they write a life insurance policy is that the client will die too soon, while the risk when they write a lifetime income annuity is that the client will live too long. Because they are on both sides of longevity risk, the company can neutralize or even eliminate longevity risk. In doing so, they can provide you with the benefits you need and would not be able to have on your own.

Know Your Options

Although it may seem that we are steering you away from term insurance and favouring the permanent life insurance alternative (which, again, is not our opinion, but a conclusion based on cold, hard facts that we will share with you below), it is imperative that you know what your options are. Remember, doing your due diligence is an essential part of structuring a successful retirement plan. Term and permanent life insurance are both products based on your life expectancy, and they each come with entirely different benefits, policies, upsides, and downsides and should be used to cover off completely different risks. Here is a rundown of what you should know about each.

Term Life Insurance

Choosing term life insurance is like renting a house. Instead of buying it outright, or making payments on it until it is yours for good, you pay a monthly rent to ensure you will have a home for the time you need one. Likewise, with term insurance, you make premium payments for a fixed amount of coverage (your death benefit) within a specific period of time. If you die during that period—usually between one and 20 years, depending on your age—your family gets to collect your death benefit. If you die after your term coverage has ended, they do not.

Term insurance is, essentially, rented insurance; it does not cover you for your entire life, but you are guaranteed coverage for a specific period of time, as long as you pay your premiums in the most cost-effective way. One of the upsides of term insurance is that you can avoid paying large lump sums and instead pay smaller premiums on a monthly or quarterly basis. Conversely, you must continue to buy new term insurance policies as your coverage runs out at the end of each period—and premiums, or cost for each new term policy rises with your age. The premiums increase slowly at first, but rise quickly to the point where you will have to drop the insurance because the premiums are just too expensive.

Here's why: life insurance is a product based on your life expectancy. As you get older, your life expectancy changes, and so must your term life insurance policy. There are several types of term insurance. A 10-year term is one of the most typical policies in Canada, and it will typically be one of the cheaper policies available. Under this policy, the term premium stays the same for the first 10 years, after which it is advised that you let the policy go and re-apply for a new term. If you are uninsurable for any reason you can keep your current policy, renewing the existing policy for another 10 years but the cost goes up exponentially. There are also 20-year, and even 30-year term policies. With these term policies, you will pay the same premium for the entire 20- or 30-year term. In effect, you will overpay for the first half of the term and underpay for the rest of the term. While these policies may seem like a good deal they are almost a guaranteed money-loser once you consider the lapse rates of term products. The lapse rate is the number of term policies cancelled prior to expiration. With lapse rates well over 50% at 10 years, all of those people paid more than they should have. If you really believe in level premium term, why not level the premium to age 100? That is, after all, precisely what a permanent life policy can offer (see next section).

123 Sample Insurance Premiums By the Numbers

Age	Women		Men	
	$250,000	$500,000	$250,000	$500,000
30	$14	$21	$17	$26
35	$14	$21	$17	$26
40	$16	$25	$21	$34
45	$19	$35	$29	$50
50	$26	$55	$40	$75

Source: WinQuote, 2014

Many people, especially in the past few decades, have claimed just this sort of common sense when explaining their decisions to opt for term life insurance. Why pay more money for unending coverage when all you want is to ensure that your life insurance holds up until your children are self-sufficient, or your mortgage is paid off? This mindset might have been sharp 20 years ago, but today it faces a harsh reality check as the age at which a young adult's self-sufficiency kicks in continues to rise dramatically and your expenses or living costs limit your ability to pay off your mortgage as soon as you would like.

Your retirement money is yours—not your children's. You have done more for them than they probably know, and retirement is a time to focus on yourself. Still, more than half of today's young people (the Gen-Y'ers who make up the largest chunk of the Canadian population since Baby Boomers) move back home after graduating from university. In 2007, a Newsweek article on the embattled future of retirement cited research that showed senior citizens in over 21 countries were giving more money to their kids than they received each year. This same article told of something even more relevant to your own retirement plan: in North America, 28% of 22- to 29-year-olds depend on money from their parents to cover "major expenses." Here is our advice: let life insurance handle your legacy to your children so you do not have to sacrifice your own happiness and retirement pleasure to help your kids out while you are alive. If your children are guaranteed money in the future in the form of a death benefit, their immediate and financial planning needs will be alleviated and you will be able to exercise your right to use your money the way you have always wanted to.

That said, even if you are going to take the term insurance route and plan to cancel when your children do not need monetary support anymore, you are looking at a long duration of premiums and term renewals. In addition, the chances that you will die while covered by your term insurance are spectacularly low. Think about this: only about 1% of people with term life insurance policies actually die within their term of coverage. That means that 99% of people with term policies die outside of their period of coverage, leaving their spouses and children behind with no death benefit at all.

Although it is losing ground, choosing the term insurance path, then dropping coverage at around age 60, still remains a popular course of action. Consider the story of Paul and Stacey Brush. Both are 35, and they have a 2-year-old son, Dylan. The Brushes envision their only child striding across the stage and receiving his diploma from the dean of a well-respected university—20 years from now. Estimating their future expenses with inflation in mind, they decide they need to provide at least $250,000 for his university costs in case something happens to them. They take out a 20-year term life insurance policy with a $300,000 death benefit for the cost of $250 a year. Paul and Stacey can rest easy knowing Dylan will have enough money to pay for University, no matter what happens to them in the next two decades.

The problem with the logic of this scenario—which, no doubt, is reality for many people—is that now, more than ever, life insurance is not just about paying for university or ensuring the well-being of your family if you die prematurely. A June 2011 article in Kiplinger's magazine heralded a new era of "common sense" when it comes to life insurance and retirement, noting that, in the past, "with the mortgage paid and the kids on their own, common sense suggested you could safely let your insurance expire". This is not so, anymore. Life insurance needs are no longer temporary, like funding Dylan's university education or paying off the mortgage. Your life insurance needs are permanent. Longer life expectancies, no pensions, and greater expenses eating into personal assets have created a retirement revolution. Leading you safely out of the frenzied upheaval: the permanent life solution.

Permanent Life Insurance

With permanent life insurance, you do not rent the home— you buy it. No one can take it away; it is yours for the long haul. The kind of life insurance you own for life.

The price is more than the cost of term insurance, but a permanent life policy can be bought at an optimal rate if you pay a lump sum. Other options include a series of level premium payments either monthly or annually over the course of a few years or your lifetime until you pay off the full amount.

There are several types of permanent life insurance. Whole life is the oldest variation and has proven to be a bellwether policy in good times and bad. Although less popular today, it is not because of poor performance. In fact, whole life insurance policies have done just the opposite. If you were to ask a handful of wealthy people what the best investment they have made over the past 15 or 20 years has been, many would say their whole life policy. Most insurance companies sell a variation of whole life. There are two different types of insurance companies that sell whole life insurance: mutual insurance companies and stock insurance companies. Mutual insurance companies are owned by their policy owners. As such, they pay dividends, not to stockholders (since there are none), but to the holders of "participating policies". Whole life is a participating policy. One reason whole life sales have decreased is that the number of mutual companies has been drastically reduced. A stock insurance company has to pay dividends to its shareholders. These shareholders do not want large sums of money paid to policyholders, so whole life appears much less attractive to them. There are a number of other reasons why whole life sales have decreased, mostly dealing with profit margins, reserve requirements, and other such complications. The main reason, though, is that there are less than a handful of mutual companies remaining.

Regardless, market trends should not deter you from purchasing a whole life policy. Whole life is actually quite an attractive form of life insurance because it has a guaranteed premium. This means premiums will never go up. Whole life also offers a guaranteed death benefit and a guaranteed cash value, so you know exactly what you are getting before you buy. In addition, the policy pays dividends each year. While most companies have paid dividends every year in the past, they are not guaranteed. Dividends can also go up or down depending on company performance and economic conditions.

It is true that you could technically save money on premium costs by buying term insurance policies in your younger years. However, your premiums would rise dramatically as you got older. Whole life premiums, by contrast, cost a little more up front but do not increase in later years. Here is what we mean:

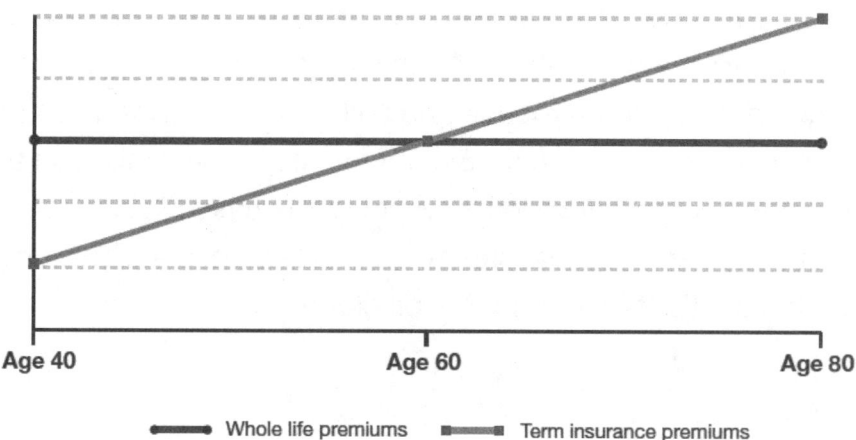

| Whole life premiums | Term insurance premiums |

It might seem like a simple trade-off—shelling out more money for more death benefit security. However, whole life insurance has other benefits up its sleeve to make you see the light. First off, let's revisit the fact that as soon as you fully pay your whole life premium (many policies offer paid up options after so many years), you are guaranteed life insurance coverage for your entire life, and your family is guaranteed a death benefit no matter when you die. It's here where we say that magic word one more time: "guaranteed". Sounds good, right? It's about to sound even better. Whole life insurance isn't just a forever-brand of term life insurance. It is a whole different animal; and, like we said, one that has a lot more benefits.

The two main parts of whole life insurance are the death benefit and the cash value. Obviously, the death benefit is what people expect from a life insurance policy, but what makes it special is that it is guaranteed for life. Essentially, for a fixed premium, which will not rise with your age if you decide to pay it off over a number of years, you are buying irrevocable and bulletproof security for your family once you are gone. But the biggest twist is this: whole life insurance does not just stash away money for your spouse and children to use when you are gone; it also builds up extra money for you to use while you are still here. This living benefit component is called "cash value", and it will be an essential part of your retirement plan. This chart might make the two-part plan a bit clearer:

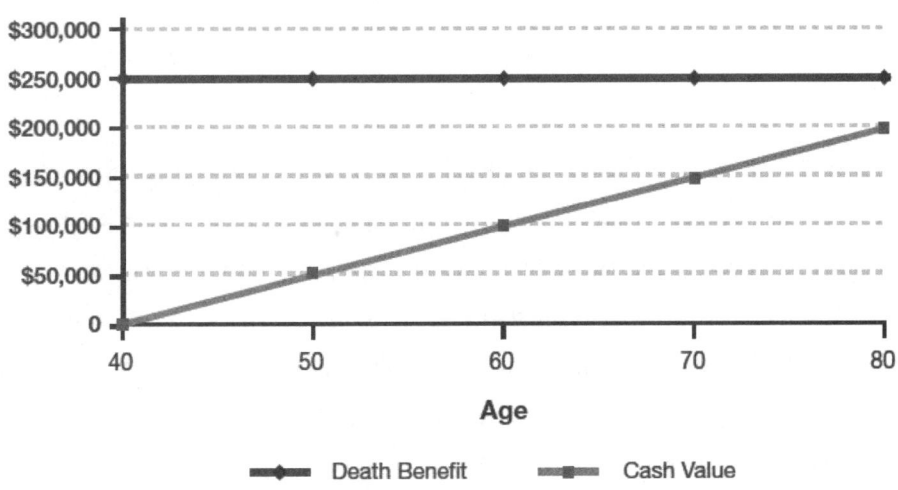

The cash value in a whole life policy is composed of two parts: a guaranteed cash value and compounded dividends. The guaranteed cash value starts very low but increases every year—regardless of market conditions or interest rates. The dividends that the policy earns can also go into the cash value. As an extra bonus, these dividends can also purchase additional paid-up insurance, so that, each year, those dividends buy more insurance which in future years will also earn dividends. So your cash value goes up every year and your death benefit rises as well. Your policy will say that dividends are not guaranteed, and they are not. However, most insurance companies have long track records for paying dividends, in some cases well over 100 years. More likely, if you buy a policy like this in a high interest rate environment, as interest rates fall, your dividend rate may not keep up with your initial projection. The company will still pay dividends, just not as high as you may have hoped. Conversely, if you buy one of these policies in a low interest rate environment, you may actually see your dividends increase over time—exceeding your expectations.

You need to note that whole life policies typically have high surrender charges in the early years. Surrender charges are fees that are assessed if you withdraw money from the cash value. These charges phase out over time. If you have made the purchase for the long term and the premium fits your budget, these charges should not alarm you. The cash value growth is tax-deferred, this means that income or growth of money earned in a permanent life insurance policy is not taxed unless it is redeemed or cashed out. The cash value in the policy can be collateralized (borrowed against) at favourable interest rates, avoiding taxation for whatever you please—emergencies, the mortgage, university tuition, that dream vacation, or in the case of Canadian billionaire Jim Pattison—it provided him the collateral to purchase his first car dealership, setting him on the path to becoming one of Canada's wealthiest people.

Back in the 1980s, another form of permanent insurance called universal life became all the rage. If you remember, interest rates paid by banks and money market funds were very high during this time. Whole life dividends seemed less and less attractive; as a result universal life was introduced. A universal life policy is really a permanent policy that combines term insurance for life with a tax-deferred, investment account. A portion of the premium covers the cost of insurance and any of the policy's fees. The two main ways to pay for universal life insurance are either a yearly renewable term where premiums increase slowly each year, or one where the premiums can be fixed and level for life (like a term 100).

The rest of the premium (if you decide to pay it) goes into an investment account within the policy, which has the ability to grow or earn interest. With the yearly renewable term option, because the actual insurance cost is less in the earlier years, you could contribute more to the cash value, allowing for compounded growth. The money can be tied to a guaranteed interest account, an index, or an investment fund, all within the universal life insurance contract. The cash value grows tax-deferred and you can take out loans, generally tax-free (loans are almost always tax-free; withdrawals are tax-free up to the adjusted cost base—typically the total sum of what you have invested). The most important part here is that you have some control over the amount of your premiums. You can raise your premiums to save more for the future, lower your premiums within the guidelines of the contract, and even stop your premiums as long as there is enough cash value to keep your monthly life insurance costs and administrative costs covered.

You can raise your life insurance death benefit (subject to company approval and/or insurability) or lower your coverage if you decide you have too much. The policy is extremely flexible. We have seen firsthand how powerful this flexibility can be. If someone loses a job, they can stop paying premiums for a while and then restart once they are back to work. We have seen businesses saved by the loan provision of the policy. However, we have also seen that flexibility allow people to hurt themselves. Because they could lower the premium, they did. But as they aged, that monthly cost of insurance rose as well (remember, one of the payment options is a yearly renewable term option in which it is part term life insurance). The premiums eventually got to the point where they could no longer afford the policy and had to let it go. Universal life premiums are typically lower than whole life premiums, but the policy can perform better the more money you put into it, depending on which investment option you choose.

However, as we know, markets do not just go up. Just as you have the unlimited upside of the market, you also have the unlimited downside. So how can we still like universal life? Simple. The people who like this product are the people who do not buy whole life because they think they can do better. Over the long run, the stock market should persevere. The policies now allow us to invest in commodities and emerging markets too through the underlying variable investment options. This policy is a wonderful alternative for the people who want to buy term and invest the difference. See, if you buy term insurance on your own, that money is gone. However, all premiums made (including those for the term costs) to the universal life policies count toward the cost basis of the policy.

Without getting too far into detail, you effectively are receiving tax-advantaged term life insurance.

There are drawbacks of course, in addition to exposure to stock market risk; universal life insurance policies carry mortality and expense charges, insurance charges, administrative charges, and possible surrender charges. However, when you compare these fees to the tax advantages gained over the life of these policies, it may make sense for some folks. The only policy that matters is the one that is in force on the day you die. You have to buy the policy that works for you.

The Investment of a Lifetime

The prospect of being able to preserve wealth within an industry as relatively safe as the life insurance industry can be somewhat of a beacon of hope for people struggling to preserve their money in an increasingly volatile market. The cash value component of whole life insurance is essentially a steady, long-term benefit simply by merit of its guaranteed dependability and security—two things that are hard to come by at any point, especially in the current economic climate.

Think of life insurance cash value as your financial bunker that can provide you with safety during difficult financial times. It is not meant to be a speedy, risky investment for you to gamble with. In fact, a whole life insurance policy gives you just the opposite: your cash value offers the certain and stable returns you need in order to take more risks with your other investments. Your whole life cash value will actually help to optimize your portfolio, as you will have more flexibility to invest and spend while maintaining your lifestyle and still leave a legacy to your loved ones—a benefit not possible under the constraints of term life insurance.

In an era of instant gratification and fast turnaround, the living benefit of whole life insurance is often overlooked in favour of riskier investments with quicker returns. A whole life policy may take more time to show its value, but your cash value can exceed the premiums you paid in around 8 to 10 years. In the long-term, whole life cash value can provide a source of funds for emergency or other needs—all it requires is a little patience.

Tax Benefits

As if these living benefits were not enough, your whole life insurance policy can also offer a slew of tax benefits. Instead of withdrawing money from your policy, you can borrow against your life insurance cash value for a source of instant credit. In less time than it would take you to merely apply for a loan from the bank, you can call your insurance company, request a cheque or wire transfer, and have your money right away.

The cash that you are borrowing has been accumulating tax-deferred, which means that, just like your RRSP, there is no tax due until you withdraw the money. In fact, you can withdraw up to the total amount of premiums paid, or borrow up to 90% of the cash value, tax-free—your insurance company will not ask you any questions or check your credit. As long as you pay back your loans when you can, your death benefit remains untouched.

This great advantage even extends past you and reaches your family and future grandchildren—there is no income tax on your death benefit, either. If structured properly, your family can also avoid probate on your death benefit.

 **How Much Life Insurance Should I Have? - By the Numbers**

The recent economic volatility and weak job market are rough on savings and retirement planning. They also complicate the issues of how much life insurance is right for you and your family, and what kind you should buy. The answer is not really how much life insurance you need—it is how much money your family will need after you are gone. Ask yourself:

- How much money will my family need after my death to meet immediate expenses, such as funeral expenses and debts?

- How much money will my family need to maintain their standard of living over the long term?

Life insurance proceeds can help pay immediate expenses, including uncovered medical costs, funeral expenses, final estate settlement costs, taxes, and other lump-sum obligations such as outstanding debts and mortgage balances. They can also help your family cover future financial obligations such as everyday living expenses, college, your spouse's retirement, and so much more.

When people sit down and figure out how much their family would really need, they are often shocked at the amount. Even families of modest incomes can have life insurance needs in the millions. Yet many only have $100,000 or $250,000 of group supplemental term life insurance from their employer. There are several ways to calculate how much is enough.

Income Replacement

Simply calculate how much money it would take to replace your income. For example, if you earn $50,000 per year, it would take $1,000,000, earning 5%, to provide that. In this low interest rate environment, you can see how easy it is to be underinsured.

Human Life Value

You will literally earn a fortune over your lifetime. If you had a machine in your garage that produced your income each year along with regular promotions and pay raises, what would it be worth? Millions of dollars! You would certainly insure that machine. Well, that machine is you. What is the present value of all of your future earnings? That is the amount that should be covered under this formula.

Financial Needs Approach

This is really a simple strategy to calculate how much coverage to buy and to form a plan that is easy to update. The idea is to assess whether you need extra coverage or different policies only after you project your life insurance needs as the sum of four categories.

- Final Expenses. A funeral, burial, and related expenses tend to cost $10,000 to $20,000. Put the number that you feel is appropriate for your family.

- Mortgages and Other Debts. Add up your mortgage balance, car loans, student loans, and any other debts that would be a burden on your survivors. They may choose not to pay off the mortgage, especially if the interest rate is low, but the money should be available so that they won't have to sell or move.

- University Expenses. This calculation can be challenging because you need to consider the cost of university at the time your kids enroll. Your spouse may also want to further their own education. Decide whether you want the insurance to cover all or a portion of the tab, and then add the amount to your life insurance calculation.

- Income Replacement. Once you cover funeral expenses, debts, and education, your family may not need to replace 100% of your income. So decide how much income your family would need and what interest rate should be used.

Add all four categories to estimate how much life insurance is appropriate, and then adjust the number to reflect any special circumstances. You might increase it if you do not have a pension, but you could decrease your coverage if your spouse earns a substantial salary. If you or a family member has a significant medical history, add more. If you are the one with the medical condition, you will find it tough to buy additional coverage later at a price you can afford.

No matter which formula you use, you will see that you need more than you probably thought.

It is acceptable to use term insurance for some of these needs. Term is very inexpensive over the short term. But you should have some permanent life insurance as well.

It may seem like life insurance could be a do-it-yourself project, but we believe there is no substitute for the guidance and assistance you will get by meeting with a qualified insurance advisor or other financial professional. So if you are serious about protecting your family's future, contact an insurance professional in your community.

Tax Diversification

We all know the importance of asset allocation and diversification of investments. When we think of diversification, we normally think of spreading our money among stocks, bonds, commodities, cash, etc. Don't put all of your eggs in one basket. By diversifying your assets, you typically smooth out the ups and downs since, historically, not all asset classes move up or down together. (More recently, we have had times when all of these assets have gone up or down together, so the search for assets that are non-correlated continues to be a very important part of diversification.)

But what about tax diversification? This is a very important concept to understand. If you think about it, most people have the majority of their investments in registered accounts. One of these registered accounts, the RRSP, offers tremendous tax advantages in the accumulation phase. The contributions are tax-deductible and offer tax-deferred growth. However, in the distribution phase, RRSPs can be a tax nightmare since all distributions are fully taxable. With all of the economic challenges facing this country, where do you think tax rates are going? With the burden of providing social programs to an increasing number of retirees and a shrinking workforce, the writing on the wall is very clear—taxes will be going up. If you agree with that proposition, our question is this: how much sense does it make to have all or most of your money in fully taxable accounts? Would it have been better to have some of that money invested where withdrawals would be tax-free?

If you could invest in the "tax perfect" retirement plan, what would it look like? It would probably include:

1. Contributions that are **tax-deductible**.
2. Accumulation that is **tax-deferred**.
3. Distributions that are **tax-free**.

Unfortunately, such a plan does not exist. But you may be able to get either 1 and 2 or 2 and 3. Increasingly, many people are liking the idea of paying taxes now on savings for retirement, knowing that they will not have to pay taxes on the growth or the distribution of that savings! Our favourite financial vehicles that allow for tax-deferred growth and tax-free withdrawals are the Tax-Free Savings Account and the cash value of life insurance. We like to say it this way: if you were a farmer, would you rather pay tax on the seed or the harvest? I think almost every farmer would rather pay tax on the seed. It works the same way with money.

Permanent life insurance that builds cash value can be a great tool in this situation. The premiums are paid with after-tax dollars. The policy's cash value grows tax-deferred and you can access cash values before or after retirement on a tax-free basis with a policy loan.

Legacy Planning

Speaking of your family, let's talk a little bit about what everyone secretly wants to know. After you are gone, what will your family legacy be? While a life insurance policy cannot determine what your entire legacy will be, it can take care of the monetary part for you (and let's hope you have the other stuff covered). Using your cash value as an estate-planning tool is one of the smartest and safest ways to add to your estate—or even create one out of thin air.

Consider the case of Joanne, a 65-year-old grandmother who wants to make sure that each of her children—and grand-children—receives a nice sum of money upon her death. Her estate is to be divided up among her five grown children, but Joanne needs to decide how to provide legacy gifts for her six grandchildren. Outside of her retirement funds, all Joanne has is a $100,000 Guaranteed Investment Certificate (GIC), which she had originally planned to use to fund her grandchildren's share of money upon her death. Here's the problem: that $100,000

GIC will essentially remain a $100,000 GIC until the day she dies, only accumulating additional value based on a meager rate of 1-2% annually for a final amount of around $110,500 in 10 years. (And don't forget taxes!)

If Joanne goes this route, each of her grandchildren will receive about $18,400 upon her death if she passes away at 75. That is all well and good, but what Joanne really wants is to increase the amount of wealth she has to distribute to her grandkids so she can ensure they all get a substantial gift when she is gone. Enter life insurance—to the rescue, once again.

By taking out a limited pay universal life insurance policy (where she will only have to pay annual premiums for three to five years until the policy is considered paid up) and naming her grandchildren as the beneficiaries, Joanne is able to purchase a policy with a death benefit more than double the amount of her premium—making her new legacy gift instantly twice the original size! Let's say this policy Joanne buys for $100,000 has a $220,000 guaranteed death benefit. Now, instead of $18,400, each of her grandkids is guaranteed $36,667—and it can all be passed along to them tax-free, outside of her estate. As if that is not enough, Joanne also retains the benefit to access all of the cash value of the policy during her lifetime in case of an emergency or any unforeseen expenses.

Some other ways that retirees use life insurance include the following:

- Using life insurance to leverage charitable giving. If a couple, aged 60, was planning on giving $50,000 to a charity, by using life insurance they could take $40,000 of the $50,000 and buy a life insurance policy that would pay the charity $150,000 upon their last death. The couple could then use the tax refund from donating the $150,000 policy to the charity and the remaining $10,000 to purchase another $100,000 life insurance policy for their estate. This would triple their $50,000 donation to their designated charity and double their $50,000 that their estate would not have even received. They would be essentially turning $50,000 into $250,000.

- Using life insurance to cover final expenses. John and Leslie, both age 70, had saved $10,000 each for their final expenses. They didn't want to be a burden on their family. Unfortunately, that $10,000 buys less and less each year. Yet they have no more money to put into their final expenses savings account. Their financial advisor recommends they each put their $10,000 into a limited pay universal life policy. This policy was guaranteed not to lapse and could be used as collateral for a loan with the insurance company at any time—so their money remained relatively liquid in case of an emergency. They now have $32,000 of final expense coverage ($15,000 on John and $17,000 on Leslie) that will be available when they die.

- Using life insurance to cover the loss of a spouse's pension upon their death. There is even a strategy called "pension maximization" where a person would select a single life payout on their pension (instead of joint life with their spouse) and use the higher pension amount (than it would have been for a joint life payout) to purchase a life insurance policy. The advantages are that if the non-pensioned spouse happened to die first, the higher pension cheque would still come for the rest of the pensioner's life. Additionally, putting the extra money in a whole life insurance policy could build cash value for an additional cheque in the future. One drawback of this approach is that the higher pension amount might not purchase enough life insurance to protect the other spouse if the pension-collecting spouse were to die. We recommend getting help from a financial advisor if you are considering this strategy.

The Longevity Gap: Avoiding Crisis for Women

As you wade into the sometimes-murky waters of choosing life insurance coverage, keep in mind that just as retirement has changed in recent years, so, in a way, has life insurance. While life insurance itself is the same old friend that has helped millions of Canadians safely ride out numerous depressions and recessions, take out loans to launch businesses, and provide for their widows or widowers, it means something different to retirees today than it has in the past.

Put simply, retirement is not what it used to be, and you will need more income over a longer period of time than your parents did. That said, you will also have a much longer retirement than your parents did. Canadians used to start working early in life, retire late, and die early. Now, they start working later in life, retire earlier, and die later. You know how we love facts; how's this for one? While your grandparents saw between 5 and 10 years of retirement on average, your generation is looking at closer to 30.

We want to stress the significance of longer life expectancy, and what it means for you and yours. Now more than ever, retirees have to rely on their personal savings and assets to ensure they can pay for basic living expenses after retiring. This fact, coupled with the startling statistics that women live an average of 5.2 years longer than men and 7 out of 10 Baby Boomer women will become widows—and live for another 15-25 years afterward—signals a looming crisis that only life insurance can ultimately resolve. If you are married, remember that there is a 50/50 chance that either you or your spouse will live to be 92 years old.

Even though women generally live longer than men, they come up short when it comes to planning ahead for their futures. When deciding on life insurance, couples need to understand the pressing need for husbands and wives to plan together for retirement, as wives will most likely be the ones reaping the consequences—and benefits—of whatever plan is chosen. A life insurance policy is the only option that guarantees to husbands that they will provide for their wives—or vice versa—when they pass away.

Essentially, when you think ahead about providing for a surviving spouse, you need to account for what income is going to die with you. If you are lucky enough to receive a pension in retirement, those cheques may stop coming after you are gone. In addition, CPP and OAS payments go down and disappear respectively with the death of a spouse. The spouse you leave behind will have reduced sources of income; this can be a devastating financial blow without proper planning.

As we have discussed in this chapter, life insurance offers you solutions to a plethora of problems faced by Baby Boomers in the next few years. One of the biggest problems of them all is the predicament Boomer women will face if they do not plan for retirement with the inevitable in mind, so that the death of a spouse does not leave them struggling and nearly broke. Life insurance is the best way to replace money that will be lost by having a reduced cheque from CPP, the loss of the OAS cheque, and it is the best way to guarantee that you and your spouse will keep receiving money for the rest of your lives.

Death is a permanent problem that we all have to face. It should be solved with permanent life insurance.

Life Insurance: The Miracle Money Machine

 Key Points from Chapter 7

1. If you were to die, how much money would be needed to allow your family to continue as if you hadn't?

2. Term life insurance is like renting. Premiums are low initially but rise significantly over time. There is no cash value. Less than 1% of term policies ever pay a death a claim.

3. Permanent life insurance is like owning. Premiums are higher, but build cash value that grows tax-deferred and can be withdrawn or borrowed out tax-free.

4. Permanent life insurance comes in 2 flavors with lots of different toppings—whole life and universal life.

5. Since women live longer than men and typically marry older men, they can look forward to a widowhood of 10, 20, even 30 years. They

will live with the consequences of how much life insurance is on the man in their life.

6. Understand the importance of tax diversification. Use TFSAs and permanent life insurance to help tax-diversify your retirement.

Chapter 8

Long-Term Care Insurance: What Is Your Plan?

No retirement plan is complete without a strategy for long-term care. For many seniors, it is the only thing they have not planned for, but it is one that could completely wipe out their entire life's work and savings. Think about that for a minute. If your house burned to the ground, it would be an emotional loss, but your insurance would cover the move or rebuild. If you totaled your car, you may have some physical injuries, but the insurance company would protect you from lawsuits and replace your car. But what would happen if you needed full-time, around-the-clock care to help you live your life? What would that cost? How long would your savings last? What would be covered under your provincial Medical Services Plan (MSP)? What would happen to your spouse and family?

The Odds That You Will Need Long-Term Care Insurance

Here are some interesting statistics:

Odds of Having a Fire?
About 3%

The odds of your home burning down between now and the day you die are about 3 out of 100 (3%), but nearly every homeowner has homeowner's insurance.

Odds of a Car Accident?
About 18%

The odds of you totaling your car between now and the day you die are about 18 out of 100 (18%), yet nearly every automobile owner carries auto insurance.

Odds of Needing Long-Term Care?
About 50%

The odds of someone 65 years old or older needing some form of long-term care before they die are about 50 out of 100 (50%), yet as of 2010, only about 385,000 Canadians were covered by long-term care insurance.

Source: StatsCan-2006, The Insurance & Investment Journal (January 18, 2013)

What is Long-Term Care?

Long-term care is defined as the type of care given when someone needs assistance with the "Activities of Daily Living" (ADL) due to an illness, accident, or old age. This assistance can be given at home or in a facility. Long-term care is not one service, but many different services that provide people the help they need when a prolonged illness or disability keeps them from being able to care for themselves. It can range from help with day-to-day activities in the home to more sophisticated services such as skilled nursing care in your home, an assisted living facility, or a nursing facility.

Activities of Daily Living (ADLs)

Bathing	Eating
Dressing	Using the toilet
Continence	Transferring (getting out of bed, chair, car, walking around, etc.)

Skilled care and custodial (or personal) care remain the most common terms used to describe long-term care and the level of assistance a person may need. Skilled care is generally needed for medical conditions that require care from a physician, registered nurse, professional therapist or other skilled medical personnel. Skilled care is usually provided 24 hours a day, is ordered by a doctor, includes some type of treatment plan and is generally provided in a nursing home.

It can also be conducted in your home with visiting nurses and other professionals. Custodial care helps a person with their activities of daily living. It is less involved than skilled care and can be performed at home, adult daycare centers, assisted living facilities, or nursing homes.

The Costs: Financial and emotional

Long-term care is not included under the Canada Health Act and, therefore, is not available to Canadians on a universal basis. Unfortunately, many Canadians continue to have the mistaken belief that all of their long-term care needs will be met by the government. While there are government programs aimed at assisting Canadians with long-term care needs, these programs vary by jurisdiction and typically are income-based. Canadians need to understand that in many cases they will be largely responsible for the cost of their long-term care needs.

Long-term care can be very expensive, and not just in financial terms. It can literally tear families apart; it can ruin the health of the caregiver in the family; and, of course, it can wipe out savings.

Institutional care can cost between $900 and $5,000 per month or more. The costs depend on the type of room selected and the level of public funding available. It also varies by province. In Ontario, for example, a private room will cost between $1,236 and $6,000 a month, while a one-bedroom apartment goes for between $1849 and $8000. In Quebec, costs range between $850 and $6,700 for a room and $750 to $2,500 for an apartment.

Hourly rates for in-home care vary between $12 and $90 per hour for domestic help with tasks such as preparing meals, or for personal and nursing care. In Ontario, the rate can range from $13 to $70 and in Quebec from $13 to $85.

Here is a hypothetical example: let's say that Mom needs long-term care assistance. For now, a few hours a day from family members or adult daycare is enough. As time goes by, Mom needs full-time care from a nursing home. Just from this example, look at the potential costs: a year of care for four hours a day, followed by a year of care for eight hours a day, followed by three years in a nursing home. Using today's costs, the total could be nearly $200,000! That leads to a couple of questions. First, where is Mom going to get that money? And second, what would your costs look like in 20 or 30 years when you might need the same type of care? The only way you will have the money for this type of expense is to plan well in advance.

When you first need long-term care, who do you think will provide care first? Of course it will be your family. They are right there; they love you and want to help you. But you have to realize the toll that providing this care will take on them. Being a caregiver is very expensive and can cause financial challenges. Your family will likely have to take time off from work and will spend their own money on all of the extras (e.g., medicine, walkers, canes, grab bars, etc.). They will have to pay someone to be with you when they cannot be there.

We have not even discussed the tremendous emotional challenges that caring for a loved one entails. Many people find themselves in the "sandwich generation" where they are not only caring for their children but their parents as well! This role reversal of children taking care of their parents is stressful and incredibly difficult. Balancing all of these priorities certainly increases both emotional and financial stress.

Providing care is a physical challenge for most caregivers. Lifting someone into or out of a bed or a bathtub, moving them from the living room to the kitchen, dressing them, and feeding them…it all takes a toll. Remember, this is full time, 24/7 care. Caregivers can suffer hernias, back problems, or other physical issues.

Long-term care really is not about you, it is about your family! Since your family is on the front lines, consider what you can do to make their lives a little easier when it comes to giving care.

Who Pays for Long-Term Care?

Many Canadians think their provincial health insurance or some government program will pay for their long-term care. The truth is that provincial health insurance and government programs may not cover all of the long-term care costs. Provincial health insurance covers medical costs such as tests, some medicines, doctor visits, hospitalization, and other specific services. What exactly is covered varies from province to province. Government programs are restricted or limited when it comes to paying for long-term care. Admissions to subsidized nursing homes are managed by the Regional Health Authority (RHA). You can apply for admission by the local RHA. The provinces' residential access policy typically ensures that seniors and people with disabilities with the highest need and urgency have priority when space in a care facility becomes available. If you or a loved one has been assessed as needing facility care, you are expected to take the first room that becomes available—regardless of how far from family the facility might be. The fees for subsidized nursing homes are based on income level. Subsidized nursing home clients will pay up to 80% of their after-tax income, subject to minimum and maximum rates.

If the government programs do not cover all the costs associated with your long-term care, what other options do you have? There are basically two options moving forward: you can pay for long-term care out of your own assets, or you can transfer the risk to an insurance company and they will pay for your care. Insurance involves pooling a small portion of your assets with a bunch of other people who, just like you, are trying to protect themselves from this same risk. Those who eventually need the assistance will get the money. Those who do not need assistance will be rewarded with the peace of mind of knowing that if they had needed the care, the money would have been available to them. This "pooling" is accomplished by buying a long-term care policy. Each month or year, you pay a premium to the insurance company in exchange for an amount of coverage.

Here is a look at your options: the first option is to self-fund. Self-funding simply means that you will pay all of the expenses not covered by MSP for your care with your personal savings and assets, at least until you spend all your money. This happens to be one of the most popular options, because if you have not made a plan for your long-term care, the government has established this plan for you. You may not like this plan, but it is the default option. Is it your best option, though? Let's step back and review your life so far. You probably have a home, a couple of cars, an RRSP or pension, and maybe some type of brokerage or savings account. You may own some GICs, annuities and some life insurance. You are trying to build some wealth, but at the same time protect yourself from large-scale disasters. You probably have homeowner's insurance, automobile insurance, maybe some critical illness insurance and disability insurance. These are all prudent ways to handle risk. If a rock goes through a windshield, you could probably afford to replace the windshield. But if your car was totaled in an accident, you would be glad you had collision coverage.

However, at retirement, some of these protections disappear. You may lose the group life insurance and disability coverage you had at work. Your other term life policy might be too expensive to keep. Your income may change from a bi-monthly paycheque to a monthly annuity and CPP/OAS cheques. As we have discussed, your strategy will probably change from accumulating assets to taking income that will last a lifetime. If you think about it, nobody lives on principal— they live on income. You will get a cheque from CPP and OAS every month and possibly a pension. Those cheques really only help to cover basic expenses, though. It is the income you receive from your investments that generate the extra income you use to really enjoy your retirement.

But what if you developed a medical condition that required

you to need long-term care? You would certainly start by using your current income, but as we discussed, given the costs involved, that would not be enough. You would then have to start spending your investment principal. However, doing so will change the entire course of retirement for both you and your spouse. Your retirement savings, which was supposed to last a lifetime, just was spent on a few years of long-term care.

The final answer? Well, you could take the chance that you might be one of the lucky ones who will not need long-term care. Yet the odds would be against you. About 50% of Canadians will need some form of long-term care before they die. If you do not have a plan to pay for these costs, the results will be devastating. So why gamble? Even wealthy people are far better off using pennies today than paying dollars tomorrow. The final funding option is long-term care insurance (LTCI). Long-term care insurance works as a partner to your provincial health insurance because your provincial health insurance may not cover all costs and may restrict your options for care. Since long-term care insurance can cover many different types of services and care, it can allow you greater choice and dignity if and when the time comes. According to the Canadian Life & Health Insurance Association, in 2010, only 385,000 Canadians were covered by long-term care insurance.

Long-term care insurance pays for services across the spectrum of care options, including:

- Home care

- Adult daycare

- Assisted living facility/residential care facility

- Nursing facility

- Hospice care

LTCI addresses some of the limitations we discussed earlier with provincial health plans. There are no hospital stay requirements and no income or asset tests to pass for receiving benefits. The policyholder must simply meet the benefit triggers identified in the policy and satisfy the elimination or waiting period indicated on the policy to qualify for benefits. These can normally be found on the Schedule of Benefits page of the policy.

Long-term care insurance provides benefits for services needed by the person listed on the policy, but can help protect the entire family as well:

Financially - by allowing you to spend money on what you want to spend it on rather than what you have to spend it on. It can leave retirement estate plans and strategies intact.

Emotionally - available resources, like the guidance of a care coordinator, can allow your family to be with you while you are receiving care rather than having to administer it themselves. This can help you stay in your home longer.

There are many stories in the media today about long-term care and a variety of companies that offer policies. How do you sort through all of the information to find the best fit for you? When shopping for long-term care insurance:

- Start with the company. Look for high financial ratings and a history of integrity. You may not need this policy for 20 or 30 years, so you want the company to be as reliable as possible. Your peace of mind will depend on the financial strength and stability of your insurer.

- Look for a comprehensive insurance policy that offers a wide range of benefits, because everyone's needs are different at the time of a claim. Some features to consider are: length of coverage (period of years or lifetime), home healthcare coverage, the daily benefit rate, and whether the payments are inflation-adjusted.

Why Buy Long-Term Care insurance?

Consider these benefits when you have a long-term care policy:

- **Retaining independence and dignity.** Seniors who have a long-term care policy retain significantly more control. They can decide to remain in their home or choose from the many assisted living facilities available. Provincial plans may not allow you much choice of how or where you will be cared for; not all care facilities are close to family, and you certainly will not have a private room.

- **Protecting the healthy spouse.** Married seniors must consider how their long-term care will affect the other spouse. For those without coverage, a spouse may be forced to pay for a caregiver from savings and the financial burden may leave minimal remaining assets for the spouse.

- **Asset protection.** An unanticipated long-term care event can literally wipe out an entire life's work. Long-term care insurance helps protect your assets from the devastating costs of an expensive illness.

- **Removal of the caregiving burden for family members.** They can spend their time enjoying your company instead of enduring the mental and physical stress that providing care can cause.

- **Peace of mind.** If you are single or do not have any close relatives nearby, long-term care insurance can reassure you that your needs are going to be taken care of. Long-term care insurance can coordinate the care you may need as well as pay for it.

What Determines the Cost of a Long-Term Care Policy?

Long-term care insurance is not as expensive as many people believe, especially in comparison to the potential cost of not having it. Here is a simple exercise for those who think it is expensive. Go on a little field trip to any assisted living facility or nursing home and sit down with some of the families that are visiting. Ask them how things are going—financially, emotionally, and health-wise. You will change your opinion pretty quickly.

The actual cost of the insurance will depend on a number of factors:

- Your age and your spouse's age at time of application

- Your health

- The amount of benefit you choose

- How long you want the benefit to pay for your care (e.g., three or five years)

- Specific policy features you select

- Any discounts you may be eligible for

There are many ways to pay for your insurance—wages, investment income—but one of the most efficient ways is using a lifetime income annuity because of the mortality credits. Do not automatically go with the lowest premium when you are out shopping. Over the past 10 years, many companies that came out with low premiums have had to significantly raise those premiums. This situation means policyholders are now in their 70s or 80s, on fixed incomes, and having to pay higher premiums. The most important thing to shop for is the strength of the insurance company and their history in the long-term care market.

A Money-Back Guarantee on Long-Term Care Insurance?

Many people do not know about this provision in some long-term care insurance policies: if a policy holder never uses their long-term care benefit, the premiums can be reverted to their family. This refund comes in the form of a death benefit. It helps overcome the objection that some people have to long-term care insurance. That objection sounds like this: "I don't want to spend my money on something I don't think I'm going to need. If I don't need the coverage, I just wasted my money on unnecessary insurance premiums."

First of all, that objection could be used for homeowner's insurance, auto insurance, or any other type of insurance. However, some long-term care policies offer a "Premium Refund Rider". This rider guarantees that you will either use the coverage while you are alive, or your family will be refunded all of your premiums at your death. Ask your financial advisor or insurance agent if that option is available for you. The option will increase the premium, but many people, especially high net-worth individuals and business owners, like it.

When should You Purchase a Long-Term Care Policy?

The simple answer is: as soon as possible. You cannot just go out and buy a long-term care policy. You have to qualify for it based on your health. Do not wait until you get a serious illness. Besides, the premiums are lower the younger you are. Delaying will make the premiums increasingly expensive, and that is if you can even still get it. There are many people out there who would happily pay 5 or 6 times your premium, if they could get the coverage. But, due to their poor health, they can no longer qualify.

Ages When People Apply	
Under 35	1%
35-44	6%
45-54	26%
55-64	50%
65-74	15%
75 or Older	2%

Source: American Association for Long-Term Care Insurance, 2008 LTCi Sourcebook

The Million-Dollar Problem

Long-term care has been referred to as a "million-dollar problem" that requires a solution. With people living longer and costs expected to go up in the coming decades, long-term care costs could represent $1 million or more in future liability for you and your family. Why face this risk alone and jeopardize your retirement and your ability to pass your estate on to your loved ones? By making a small investment now in long-term care insurance, you can solve the million-dollar problem.

Keep in mind that everyone has a plan for long-term care. If you do not think you have a plan, let us assure you that you do. Now, you may not like the plan that has been set up for you, but you do have a plan: pay until you run out of money, then become a ward of the state, most likely in a nursing home. Our plan is simple: We want to stay in our home until the day we die. We will not have to go into a nursing home. The nurse has to come to us. And our favorite part—we get to pick the nurse! We have a long-term care policy with a home healthcare coverage—we get to stay in our home!

We'll bet that is the plan that you would prefer as well. But as we said—you cannot just buy a long-term care insurance policy. You have to qualify for it with your health. You cannot wait until you have a serious medical condition or you are unable to take care of yourself without assistance. Today is the healthiest day of your life. Every day from here on out, we will all be just a little older and less healthy than the day before. The time to get your policy is today. Do not wait. Long-term care insurance should be purchased in your 40s or 50s. That way you will have a plan that allows you to control your care and provide a solution to the million-dollar problem.

OTHER LIVING BENEFITS:

Much like long term care insurance, most people don't have a financial or an emotional plan for poor health. Overcoming financial hardship and its emotional stress after suffering from cancer, a heart attack or a stroke is not easy. While Canadians have universal health care that will pay most medical bills, who pays your other bills? Your mortgage, utilities, car payments, prescriptions?

If you are still working, hopefully, you have arranged for some form of income replacement should you become disabled. One of the best ways to explain the importance of this income is the Job A the Job B example:

Job A pays you an annual salary of $75,000. Should you become sick or injured and be unable to work, you get $0 income and will have to rely on your savings or government benefits to continue to pay for a roof over your head and put food on the table. Not the best option we can think of but if you haven't planned for income replacement, these are your only options.

Job B pays you $72,500 a year but if you become sick or injured it will provide you with 66% of your pre-tax income. A much better choice, whether you are single or if you are responsible to people other than yourself.

If you chose Job B, congratulations, you just made the decision to have disability insurance. Disability (or income replacement) insurance is important if you are working, but is only designed to replace lost employment income - the minute you stop working, is the minute you are ineligible to apply for this type of insurance.

Remember when we said that the most important years of a retirement plan are the 5 years before retirement and the 5 years right after you retire? This is Prudential's Retirement Red Zone discussed in chapter 2. When do you think is the most likely time for you to get sick? It's right around now.

Another type of coverage that will protect your assets is critical illness insurance. If you are diagnosed with a critical illness, this insurance pays out a tax-free lump sum of money. The money can be used for anything, it's up to you. This means that your retirement portfolio can remain intact should you suffer an illness that requires you to spend money you may not otherwise have.

The benefit of critical illness insurance is that its payout will provide you with options. To explain more about the coverage, what it does and why you need it, we have included an article by Micheline Varas. Micheline is one of Canada's top living benefits specialists and is the Senior Vice-President, Living Benefits for Customplan Financial Advisors. She knows her stuff:

During the second half of the last century, the incidence of major diseases experienced a dramatic shift. This change was mostly due to variances in lifestyle such as stress, smoking, obesity, lack of exercise, and so on. As a society we experience far higher occurrences of cancers, heart attacks and strokes today than we did a century ago. This has magnified medical advances and treatments which have been instrumental in prolonging life – people no longer die as quickly... we're surviving! Today we are living far longer lives than generations before us, but do so while coping with chronic conditions that once were primary causes of death. Physicians measure survival in quantity of life, and the quality of life is often overlooked. We seem to have traded death (or mortality) for disability (or morbidity).

The financial burden on those who are seriously ill (and of course on their families, businesses, etc.) can be onerous if not devastating. We overlook the expenses of specialized or holistic medications, treatments, therapies and rehabilitation often not covered by either government or private plans. When faced with one of these life-altering diseases, life and disability insurance products are not the answer. Life insurance is only effective once we succumb to the illness, while disability insurance is structured to replace lost income. Witnessing the financial impact of illnesses led to the creation of Critical Illness Insurance by Dr. Marius Barnard.

Dr. Marius Barnard was a member of the team (which was headed by his brother, Dr. Christiaan Barnard), that performed the world's first human heart transplantation. Dr. Marius Barnard was so impressed by his patients' financial hardship after he had treated their critical illnesses, that he convinced the South African insurance companies to introduce a new type of coverage. Barnard argued that, as a medical doctor, he can repair a man physically, but only insurers can repair a patient's finances "... although (patients) lived longer, financially they were destroyed. It became obvious to me that my patients did not only need insurance because they were going to die, but because they were going to live". Barnard experienced the impact his patients' financial problems had in their recovery and physical health. Critical illness insurance was not the genius of insurance company, actuary or sales team, but of a cardiac surgeon who recognized the need for "dread disease" coverage. On August 6, 1983, the first "dread disease insurance" policy emerged in South Africa. History lesson out of the way, we can now focus on financial well-being!

Though a healthy lifestyle is instrumental in reducing potential health risks, a critical illness can affect anyone regardless of age. Though something none of us wishes to face, it happens; often when we least expect it. According to a 2009 survey conducted by Munich Reinsurance Co., the "average" age of people who make a critical illness insurance claim is 50 for men and 48 for women. This realization can help us to look to our personal situation from a different perspective. Heart disease, stroke and cancer are the leading health issues facing Canadians today:

- *40% of Canadian women and 45% of Canadian men will develop cancer during their lifetimes.*

- *It is estimated that there are over 70,000 heart attacks in Canada each year.*

- *Every 10 minutes, one person in Canada has a stroke and after age 55, the risk of stroke doubles every 10 years.*

- *1 out of 2 heart attack victims is under the of 65 and 95% survive their first attack.*

The good news is more Canadians than ever are surviving life-altering illnesses:

- *Cancer mortality rates are declining for males under the age of 80 and for females under the age of 70.*

- *In recent years, the rate of survival among patients hospitalized for a heart attack has increased to 92%.*

- *80% of Canadians hospitalized for stroke each year leave the hospital alive[5].*

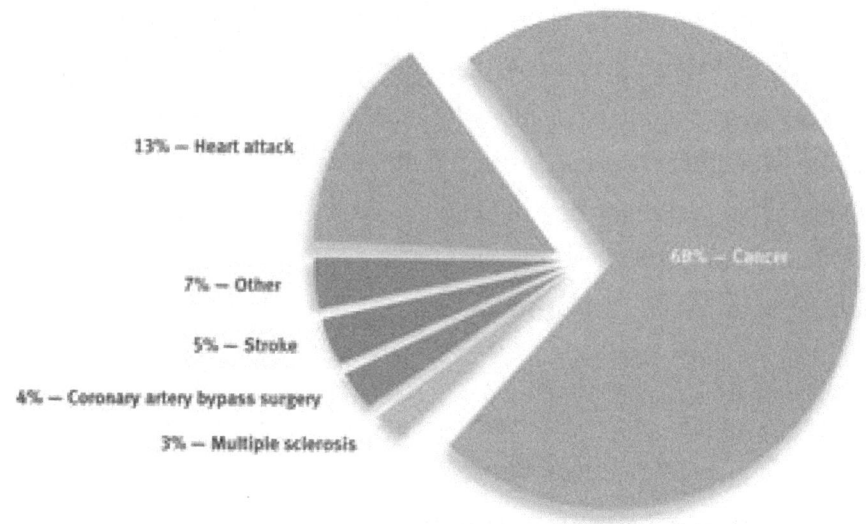

13% — Heart attack

7% — Other

5% — Stroke

4% — Coronary artery bypass surgery

3% — Multiple sclerosis

68% — Cancer

* Source: Munich Reinsurance Company, 2010 Individual Insurance Survey.

Enduring a critical illness can be one of the greatest challenges in life. Everyone knows of a friend, family member or colleague who has had a heart attack or undergone cancer treatment. Though they may have survived, returned to work, and resumed "normalcy" in their daily life, both their life and that of their family, friends and associates have been adversely affected.

There are many factors that come into play when dealing with a critical illness. These can include the stress of the diagnosis, the physical and mental toll of the illness, the impact of lost wages, medical and rehabilitation costs, personal day-to-day needs and the long-term security of our family and perhaps our business.

So what is Critical Illness Insurance? It is a type of protection that provides immediate funds to you (usually when you survive 30 days) upon the diagnosis of a covered condition such as cancer, stroke or heart attack. It's often referred to as a "Living Benefit" which can financially assist you, your family and your business through the hardships associated with a critical illness. Unlike other insurances that are based on income replacement should you be injured or become ill, Critical Illness Insurance provides lump-sum of tax-free capital that can be used any way you choose without claw-backs or restrictions to other benefits.

Keeping finances in mind, it's important for us to look more closely as to how our life would be affected if we were to suffer from a critical illness. Our finances could be impacted by: loss of income or business, special rehabilitation expenses or out-of-country expenses (or medical treatments available in another province), in-home nursing (a child care provider or housekeeper), the need for equipment (wheelchair, home care bed or scooter) or home or car modification costs (widening doors, altering bathrooms, kitchens, entrances or changing floor surfaces) and perhaps a high liability exposure (such as lines of credit or business loans).

Proceeds from a critical illness payout can be used to top-up income derived from a disability plan (should you have insufficient or off-the-job coverage) or reduce or even eliminate outstanding debt such as a mortgage, car loans and credit cards. There is a strong chance that you will be away from work for a significant amount of time or perhaps lose your job altogether, so the lump sum benefit provides options at a very difficult time. The benefit can be used to protect a child's education fund or retirement savings as most individuals would need to rely on RRSPs (or home equity) to fund unforeseen medical and non-medical expenses. We could also look to off-setting the cost of medical deductions attributed to tax returns.

If you are a business owner, the policy benefit can be used to maintain continuity, hire help, protect business income and avoid the need to be forced to sell in order to meet a called bank loan. In the corporate market, the policy guarantees uninterrupted

income flow of the company due to the illness of a key employee, assists in finding their replacement, and avoids havoc within operations or potential downturn of stock prices due to revenue loss. Critical Illness Insurance can protect shareholders, key persons and fund Buy/Sell agreements.

Will other plans provide coverage for you in the event of a critical illness?

In choosing any type of insurance, it is crucial to understand how it works. With critical illness insurance we have already determined that it pays a lump sum should you survive a covered critical illness. Once the survival period (30 days) has been satisfied, the funds are paid directly to you and you are free to use the money in any way you see fit! There is one exception at the beginning of the coverage period. Should you have symptoms or be diagnosed with cancer within the first 90 days of coverage, no payment will be made. The contract remains in force, however, it will exclude cancer coverage. It is your responsibility to advise the insurance company (or your advisor) within 6 months of this discovery or the policy can become void. Covered conditions are listed within the individual policies. While some contracts cover only the primary conditions (cancer, stroke, heart attack and coronary artery bypass), others' lists can be extensive. Each covered condition

		YES	NO
Life Insurance	Will it pay in case you die for your dependents/business to be financially taken care of?	X	
	Will it pay for your recovery of a critical illness?		X
Disability Insurance	Will it ensure an income to cover every day expenses if you cannot work due to an injury/illness?	X	
	Will that income be sufficient to cover extraordinary expenses that may result from a critical illness?		X
Health Plan	Will it reimburse most covered medically related expenses?	X	
	Will it cover expenses if you choose to go out-of-province for a non-emergency or experimental procedure?		X
Critical Illness	Will it provide funds if you are diagnosed with and survive a covered condition?	X	
	Will you be able to use the money any way you choose to enhance your recovery?	X	

has its own specific definition which outlines the criteria for determining the proper diagnosis of that condition.

Choosing insurance contracts is never an easy feat and Critical Illness Insurance is no different! Critical illness policies, like life insurance policies can vary in their durations and there are renewable term plans, level premium term plans and permanent plans. It is available in individual and group insurance *as well as creditor products sold through banks or lending institutions. It can sometimes be offered on a "guaranteed issue" basis where some companies will allow for coverage to be issued without medical underwriting. These may include pre-existing condition limitation clauses or other restrictions.*

Policies differ in their guarantees, features and benefits. The last of these can include early assistance (whereby a percentage of the benefit is paid upon early detection/diagnosis of certain conditions); assistance services (such as Best Doctors, Daily Living Assistance, Emotional Support Help-lines, etc.); Return of Premium riders (upon either no incurrence of claim or upon death); conversion options, loss of independence riders and the list goes on!

No matter what plan you have in place, nothing can prepare you for the emotional and financial burden associated with suffering a critical illness. Dealing with the illness is difficult enough; the additional stress of its financial impact, distressing. Proper planning will allow you and your advisor to discuss the vital role of critical illness insurance will play in your overall financial plan. It can protect your personal and business needs, cover your mortgage or fund a buy/sell agreement between business partners. It can also protect your assets, your retirement plan and your child's education. You retain control – of yourself, your lifestyle and your financial future, maintaining dignity and independence. With an average claim age of 48 to 50, from a financial standpoint alone, critical illness can deplete your retirement plan. In summary, critical illness provides a lump sum of money that can be used for anything 30 days after the diagnosis and survival of a covered illness. You won't need to worry financially, just deal with what's most important ... your health.

Critical illness insurance is not unique to Canada, but Canada's products are unique. What sets them apart are premium guarantees. There are two different types of individual coverage: term and permanent. Within the term options, Canada differentiates itself from the rest of the world by offering guaranteed renewal rates. This means that when you purchase a 10 or 20 year term critical illness policy, you know exactly how much you are going to be paying now and on each term renewal should you become uninsurable in the future. Historically, the guaranteed renewal rates have been fairly close to the actual renewal rates.

Also offered by the Canadian marketplace is permanent critical illness insurance. This is typically called Level to age 65, Level to age 75 or Level to age 100. For those wanting to prepay their coverage, there are alternatives which will allow you to purchase a permanent policy in 10 to 15 years.

Some permanent critical illness insurance plans also offer a rider referred to as "return of premium on expiry". Basically, if you do not get sick and make it to the end of the level period (or sometimes a defined number of years), you get all your money back. This is almost like betting the insurance company that you won't get sick. If you are diagnosed with a critical illness, you receive the payout; if not, you get all your money back. Not a bad option, especially if you are trying to protect your retirement fund while you're in the Retirement Red Zone.

As the "return of premium on expiry" is a rider, there is an additional cost, but if you don't think anything will happen to you, it can be worthwhile. Another option is the "return of premium on death". This pays back to your estate or your named beneficiaries, all paid premiums should you die prior to the critical illness insurance pay out.

If you choose the "return of premium on expiry" option and do not get sick, all you have foregone is the interest on the cost of the rider.

Let's look at Susan's situation. She is a single 50 years old, with two children in their mid-20's who have finally moved out. Susan has 10 more years to work but wants to ensure nothing will negatively affect her retirement plans and goals. Critical illness is explained as independent personal coverage. Her life insurance policy will provide for her children, but a critical illness plan looks after Susan! Should she become critically ill, she will receive a lump sum ensuring she has money to take care of herself financially.

Susan is thinking about the return of premium option so we broke out the math behind her two choices. You know by now that we are fans of mathematically proven, scientific fact. For the sake of these quotes, we have included the return of premium on death in both scenarios.

The two choices that we provided her with are Level to 75 without return of premium. The monthly cost of this policy without the return of premium option at expiry rider is $140.00 per month. If Susan gets sick at any point between now and 75 years old (not including the initial 90 day coverage exclusion) she will receive a tax-free cheque for $100,000 from the insurance company to do with whatever she feels is most important to her inclusive of seeking private care in the U.S., travel once she recovers or paying off her mortgage. If Susan does not get sick by age 75, the critical illness insurance policy then terminates and she is returned all premiums she paid.

The second option we presented her with was a Level to Age 100 policy with a return of premium option starting after 15 years. This option covers her for the most crucial years of critical illness occurrence and at age 65 she can cancel the policy altogether (at which time she would receive 100% of the premiums paid back to her tax-free). It provides protection, lessens her premium paying years and supplements her retirement income if she doesn't get sick. The monthly cost for the Level to age 100 with return of premium is $340 per month and though slightly more, she will be paying 10 less years of coverage. So, if at age 65 Susan has not been diagnosed with a covered critical illness, she has the option to surrender the policy and receive back all money she had paid. If Susan becomes critically ill, she receives a tax free cheque in the amount of $100,000.

Here are the numbers that we looked at for Susan:

- $42,000 is the life time cost for a Level to 75 policy without return of premium on expiry

- $61,200 is the cost to age 65 for Level to Age 100 policy with return of premium on expiry after 15 years

- Interest forgone if she had purchased the Level to Age 100 policy without the return of premium on expiry and had invested the difference at 3% is $5,871.59.

Either option provides her with the same benefit she needs at a very difficult time in her life. Like long term care insurance critical illness coverage is for those who are presently healthy. You need to qualify medically for most plans. The odds of being diagnosed with a critical illness are increasing and the financial hardship and stress can often be overwhelming. Why not protect your health and your retirement portfolio at the same time with permanent critical illness insurance?

Long-Term Care Insurance: What Is Your Plan?

 Key Points from Chapter 8

1. No retirement plan is complete without a plan for long-term care.

2. The odds of you losing your home to fire are 3%; totaling your car, 18%; but needing long term care before you die, more than 50%!

3. Long-term care insurance provides help with the activities of daily living. These expenses are not all covered by provincial health plans.

4. Long-term care is very expensive. It can also cause physical and emotional stress to family members who are giving the care.

5. A long-term care insurance policy gives the control back to you. You can stay in your home, utilize assisted living, adult daycare, or other options. Money is provided to modify your home to make it easier and safer to stay at home.

6. You cannot buy a long-term care policy—you have to QUALIFY for it. You qualify for it with your health.

Chapter 9

Estate Planning: How Will You Be Remembered?

Just like how no retirement plan is complete without a plan for long-term care, no retirement plan is complete without an estate plan. We have witnessed firsthand many disasters suffered by the families of those who did not have an estate plan. If you think about it, we have already discussed a number of very simple ways to improve your estate plan.

In Chapter 3, we met the 83-year-old gentleman from the United States who simply wanted a guaranteed paycheque for the rest of his life. When he died, he wanted his wife to get that same cheque. When she died, he wanted his son to get that cheque, then his daughter-in-law, and, eventually, his granddaughter. He could use an annuity to achieve his goals. That annuity was a form of a very simple estate plan. It was not a complete plan by any means, but it was better than what many people have done. If you remember, there were two questions we always ask anyone who inquires, "Where do you want your money to go when you die?" and, "What do you want your money to do for you while you're alive?"

In Chapter 5, we met the 75-year-old grandfather who wanted to do something special for his granddaughter. We recommended a joint lifetime income annuity that paid him a cheque every time his granddaughter had a birthday. When he died, she continued to get that same cheque every birthday for the rest of her life (she would never forget her favourite grandpa!). Ultimately, when she died, her daughter got the $50,000 tax-free death benefit (she would never forget her great-grandpa, either). This approach is a form of estate planning as well. A big part of estate planning has to do with gifting strategies—how can you transfer your wealth in the most efficient manner possible?

If that sounds familiar, it is: we said those words back in Chapter 6 when we discussed life insurance—life insurance is a wealth transfer vehicle. Estate planning is all about wealth transfer. In that same chapter, we looked at how to utilize life insurance in order to create an estate worth two or three times more than what you would have left to your loved ones without it.

This book is loaded with simple ideas about estate planning. This chapter will round out our thinking on the subject. It is not a technical chapter going into exhaustive detail on extremely complicated estate planning strategies. It will be more of an overview of how to create an estate if you need one, and some ways to transfer an estate if you have one. The more money you have, the more complex your estate can be and the more help you need. A good estate plan is not a do-it-yourself project. A good estate planning lawyer and a financial professional are worth their weight in gold, and they can help you save far more in taxes and probate costs than you would ever pay them in fees.

Creating an Estate

Those of you who do not have a significant estate may be thinking, "This chapter has nothing to do with me. I can barely make it on my own." Others of you may not have any family to leave anything to. Still others may really want to leave some money to loved ones, but just do not know how to do it. There is a vehicle that offers tremendous leverage and can actually create a very large estate with a small amount of money—money that can go to the surviving family, a long serving trusted employee, a favourite grandchild, or even a favourite charity. We are talking about life insurance. Life insurance is the only financial product that can literally create a multi-million dollar estate out of thin air. A person could make a single premium payment to a life insurance company and if a bus hits him later that afternoon, the family could receive a multi-million dollar death benefit.

History is filled with stories of people who have made a huge difference to their families, universities, churches, and other charities with large life insurance death benefits. If you have not built the estate that you had hoped while you were working, it is not too late to create a financial legacy by using life insurance.

Estate Planning Objectives

"Thrift is a wonderful virtue, particularly in an ancestor."

- Mark Twain

Estate planning involves leaving your property to your loved ones and/or charitable causes after your death. You may even transfer some assets while you are still alive to take advantage of certain tax exemptions and to provide assistance when needed (e.g., your grandchildren's college tuition). The first step is to get a handle on what you own, which includes everything from real estate, stocks, mutual funds, life insurance policies, retirement accounts, and bank accounts, to personal property such as cars, jewelry, or art. Second, you need to start thinking about who should get what assets and when. Then you can consider the best planning approach to see that it all happens.

Here is a simple exercise. Take a few minutes and just think about your death. If you were not here, who would it impact and how? What would happen if your paycheque, pension or OAS cheque stopped? Who would do all of the things you do every day? Who would handle the financial affairs, mow the lawn, and take care of the kids (or your parents)? Are there important people in your life for whom you want to do something special? Any favourite charities? Today, start by putting together a plan to have your money do the things you want it to do when you die. You cannot take your money with you. It all stays here. What do you want that money to do? How do you want to be remembered? Think about these issues as we look at some basic estate planning documents and how they are used.

Estate Planning Documents

WILLS

Remember in the last chapter when we said, "Everyone has a plan for long-term care. If you think you don't have a plan, you're wrong. You do have a plan—you just won't like your plan"? The same can be said for estate planning! If you die without a will, you are said to have died intestate. Intestate means that you will have no input in how your estate is distributed by a probate court. The province will decide how your estate is divided and distributed. The intestate succession laws vary from province to province but have similar elements.

A will is the most basic estate-planning document. A will typically includes:

> a. A description of who you are (enough information to clearly identify that this is your last will and testament).

> b. The names of your beneficiaries (which can be both people and institutions) and enough information (addresses, dates of birth, etc.) that whoever is reading the will can clearly identify them.

> c. The name of the person you are appointing as executor to manage your estate and make sure the assets get distributed to the beneficiaries (it is a good idea to appoint a secondary executor in

case the first is unable or unwilling to discharge the duties). You should also get the approval of the person you are appointing in advance.

d. Your directions regarding who will care for your children, your parents, or anyone else for whom you are legally responsible.

e. How you want your assets distributed when you die. You can make both specific bequests (e.g., I leave my diamond ring to my niece) and general bequests (e.g., I leave one-third of my estate to my son).

Although a will seems like a simple enough document and the Internet is loaded with do-it-yourself "will kits", this is much too important of a document to not have it prepared and reviewed by a lawyer. Wills can be disputed. The laws on what constitutes a valid will vary from province to province. Spend a few bucks more to make sure your will is exactly the way you want it to be.

One final point about wills is that they provide for the distribution of assets that go through probate proceedings. Assets that pass outside of probate are not distributed according to your will.

TRUSTS

The most popular document for people who have significant assets is a trust. If you do not have much money, you may not need a trust. A simple will may suffice. We say "may" because there are many people who have simple estates who prefer to have a trust anyway because of the privacy and control it affords. A trust is a legal document to hold and manage your property and assets for your beneficiaries. You can transfer some or all of your assets into the trust. The trust will ensure that your assets will be managed and distributed according to your wishes after you die.

Just like a will, a trust has several components:

a. The person setting up the trust (often referred to as the trustor, settlor, or grantor).

b. The objective of the trust.

c. The type of trust.

d. The property or assets that are put into the trust (known as trust property).

e. The beneficiaries (the people or institutions that will receive some or all of the trust property or otherwise benefit from the trust).

f. The trustee (the person in charge of the trust).

g. The distribution rules (i.e., how often money will be paid out). For example, beneficiaries could receive income from the trust, or they could have the ability to tap some of or the entire principal for certain purposes.

A trust, like a will, is not a do-it-yourself project. There are several different types of trusts, so make sure that you are using the appropriate type. Entire books have been published that explain the details on each of these trusts. Financial advisors and lawyers can go on and on about their favorite ones and why, and it is important to get advice from a qualified professional when setting up a trust.

Why set up a trust? Trusts have several important advantages that you should understand. These benefits include:

a. Avoiding probate. By keeping your assets and property out of your probate estate, you can skip many of the hassles, costs, and privacy concerns that are a part of the public probate process.

b. Protecting your estate (and your beneficiary's estate). A trust can protect assets from lawsuits, divorce, spendthrift relatives, and much more.

c. Provide funding for grandchildren's education. You can designate funds to be used for certain purposes.

d. Leaving a legacy that is handled exactly the way you want. You can literally "control from beyond the grave". Assets are managed and distributed according to your instructions long after you are gone.

MEDICAL DOCUMENTS:
DEALING WITH INCAPACITY

In addition to distributing assets at death, a complete estate plan should also include documents to follow in the event that you become incapacitated through illness and are unable to handle financial and medical decisions. There are two basic documents you should have in place: an enduring power of attorney and healthcare directive.

An enduring power of attorney allows the person you designate to handle your financial affairs just as you would, including accessing bank accounts and paying bills. The power is "enduring" in the sense that it continues in the event that you become incapacitated due to physical or mental illness. It is a good idea to have this document because otherwise your family would have to go to court to appoint a guardian or conservator, which can be expensive and time-consuming. The person you select should be responsible and trustworthy.

A healthcare directive is similar to the enduring power of attorney, except that it allows the person named in the document to make medical care decisions in the event that you become incapacitated. These decisions pertain to treatment, tests, and medication, as well as life-prolonging procedures. You can give specific instructions to the agent regarding certain treatments that must be followed (e.g., no feeding tubes), or you can give your agent more flexibility. This document can help to prevent conflicts among relatives over medical decisions and will help expedite your medical treatment.

TO PROBATE OR NOT TO PROBATE...

Probate is the process whereby a provincial court manages the distribution of your property to your beneficiaries. If you have a will, the court will follow your distribution plan. In the event that you do not have a will, the assets are distributed according to the laws of intestacy in your province. However, not all assets have to pass through probate. With proper planning, most assets can pass outside of probate. The advantages of avoiding probate include not having to pay your provincial probate fee (for example, probate in BC is 1.4% on estates over $50,000), lower fees to lawyers and accountants, fewer delays in getting assets to beneficiaries, and keeping your distribution decisions private. There are several main techniques for avoiding probate. Trusts, discussed above, are one. Holding your investments inside segregated funds is another. There are two other ways as well:

- **Joint With Rights of Survivorship (JWROS):** Ownership will pass automatically to the surviving joint owner without going through probate. To use this technique, you would simply have to add another person to your real estate deed, bank account, or other assets. The risk here is that it opens your assets to unlimited liability from both parties. For example, if you named your daughter as joint owner on your property and her husband owned a business. If that business went bankrupt, your assets could and most likely would be seized. A joint with rights of survivorship situation can be a very effective estate-planning tool but should only be entered into after understanding and considering all of the potential risks.

- **Assets with named beneficiaries:** Ownership passes directly to the named beneficiary and transfers outside of probate. Examples of the types of assets with named beneficiaries include: annuities, life insurance, pensions, RRSPs & RRIFs, and TFSAs. While RRSPs and RRIFs bypass probate, the taxes owed will need to be paid by your estate on your terminal tax return because they are considered disposed of at the time of death.

By using these techniques, you can reduce or eliminate the need for probate and the associated fees and delays.

Life Insurance as a Wealth Transfer Technique

We have worked with a lot of wealthy people over the years. Whenever we get to the estate-planning portion of the discussion, clients always have a tough time understanding why they should buy a big life insurance policy. There was one case that Tom worked on in particular. Ed was a very successful rancher in the Western United States. He was worth around $15 million. We were recommending a $7 million life insurance policy to pay the estate taxes. Ed said, "I just don't want any life insurance! Heck, I'm loaded—I'm worth $15 million, why do I need life insurance? In fact, I'd have to say life insurance is the last thing I need. I think you boys are just trying to make a big commission."

This is a very common objection from wealthy people, but Tom didn't even flinch. In fact, he smiled because he knew it was coming. He just leaned forward, looked Ed in the eyes, and said, "Ed, let me be the first to agree with you. You are worth a lot of money and you are correct —you don't need any life insurance. What you need is a way to transfer your wealth to your wife and kids in the most tax-efficient manner possible—would you agree with that?" Ed said, "I guess. And that is what I thought we were going to talk about before you started pushing this life insurance on me." Tom just smiled again and said, "Ed, if we could transfer your wealth with real estate, or stocks, or bonds, or GICs or Coca-Cola cans, we would. But the tax code clearly favors one method, and that is life insurance. There is no more efficient way to transfer wealth to your heirs than life insurance. And Ed, that is not an opinion. That is a mathematical, scientific, and economic fact." Tom sat back, thinking he had done about as good a job as could be done. Yet Ed was still unconvinced.

The agent, Bob Blach, who is a friend of Tom's, reached into his bag and took out four plastic cows from a kid's farming set. He set the four plastic cows on the table. Bob said, "Ed, these are your "cash cows". This one represents all of your land. This one represents all of your buildings. This one represents all of your equipment and this one represents all of your investments and bank accounts. Now, when you die, the IRS (the U.S. version of CRA) is going to come to the farm and butcher two of these cows." They will butcher those two cows and keep all of the meat. But it doesn't have to be that way. If we took some of the milk from each of the cows, we could take out a life insurance policy that will pay the IRS when you die, allowing all of your cash cows to go to your family. Ed, the choice is yours." Tom sat back in amazement. Ed's eyes

> lit up—he got it! He understood estate planning
> through the eyes of a 6-year-old with those toy
> cows! We all learned a lot that day about story-
> telling and the power of simplicity.
>
> So, how do you want to be remembered?

A discussion of estate planning would not be complete without discussing segregated funds, which we discussed earlier.
Segregated funds have the unique characteristic of living in two
worlds at once: the investment world, where they act like mutual
funds, and the insurance world, where they are contract-based.
Segregated funds can be creditor protected if set up properly,
meaning if you were to go bankrupt, the assets held within a
segregated fund would not be seized. Segregated funds also
come with two types of guarantees: a maturity guarantee and
a death benefit guarantee. The maturity guarantee works like
this: if you hold the segregated fund for 15 years and it is worth
less than what you paid for it, you can cash it in and receive all
of your original investment back. With the death benefit guarantee, if you pass away while the value of your investment is
less than what you put in, your named beneficiaries will receive
an amount equal to what you originally invested. If you have
named beneficiaries of a segregated fund, this allows the beneficiaries to receive those assets privately and confidentially in
a way that bypasses probate.

Estate Planning: How Will You Be Remembered?

 Key Points from Chapter 9

1. No retirement plan is complete without an estate plan.

2. You can create an estate with life insurance.

3. Estate planning is all about transferring your wealth and assets to your family or favorite charity in the most tax-efficient manner possible.

4. If you were to die today, who would be impacted? How? What can you do now to limit any financial problems caused by a premature death?

5. Wills, trusts, and medical documents may all play a role in how your estate is handled.

6. Probate, capital gains and income taxes can have a significant impact on your family. These taxes must be paid promptly and have forced many families to sell property and assets at fire sale prices. Plan now to mitigate any problems.

7. Wealthy people always say, "I don't need any life insurance." They are right. However, they need a way to transfer that wealth to their family in the most tax-efficient way possible. That often leads right back to life insurance. Life insurance is the most tax-favoured wealth transfer vehicle.

Chapter 10

And They Lived Happily Ever After

We started with the question "What Happened to Happily Ever After?" Things used to be so simple. People worked for 30 or 40 years—many times with the same company—and received a very comfortable pension to last them through their retirement. Because of shorter life expectancies back then, for many, retirement was a short period of time prior to death.

Fast forward to today—people are living longer, defined benefit pensions are a faded memory of days gone by, markets are more volatile than ever, and retirement has become a scary word. The greatest risk for pension fund managers is that they will not have enough money to fund future retirement benefits claims. You need to be similarly concerned about underfunding because you are responsible for managing your own retirement plan. We talked about the risks of inflation, deflation, living too long, and withdrawing too much. It is so important to understand the power of longevity risk.

Longevity is not just a single risk in retirement—it is a multiplier of all of the other risks.

Think about it. If you only live five years in retirement, inflation really will not have much impact on your portfolio. It would not matter if you withdrew 10% per year since you would only be taking money out for five years. It would not make much difference if the market dropped 30%. None of the other risks would really matter if you died early in retirement. However, for each additional year you live, the other risks grow exponentially! If you live to be 100, almost none of the formulas used for investment simulation would provide an effective solution. Inflation could devastate your fixed income or savings accounts. Withdraw even 0.5% too much money each year and you will run out. So longevity is not simply a risk—it is a risk that makes all of the other risks very real.

The Investment Two-Step: Guaranteed Income and Inflation Protection

The solution to this dilemma is a very simple: a two-step process that is supported by math and science. Step one is to cover basic expenses with guaranteed lifetime income. First, you need to know how much money you need each month in retirement. Subtract out your Canada Pension Plan, Old Age Security and any pensions you may receive. The remaining shortfall needs to be covered by a lifetime income annuity.

Because of the mortality credits, which provide additional benefits the longer you live, only a lifetime income annuity can optimize income over the indefinite period of a human life. Dr. Menahem Yaari proved this in the 1960s. If you do not use a lifetime income annuity, one of the following will be true: you will either spend too much and eventually run out of money; or you will spend too little and never live the retirement you dreamed about.

The second step is to optimize the portfolio for inflation. This approach will be difficult for some conservative investors. If you have saved money your whole life in GICs, bank accounts, or other conservative investments, it will be difficult to suddenly invest in oil, gas, gold, real estate, stocks, ETF's, and other inflation-sensitive investments. Yet that is exactly what we are saying to do with some of your money. Remember, if all of your expenses are covered by guaranteed income, you have already removed most of the risks in retirement. You have taken care of longevity risk since you get those cheques for the rest of your life. The payments will never go down, so you have taken deflation, recession, and depression off the list. Since the returns from lifetime income annuities do not fluctuate (they have a zero standard deviation—see chart on next page), you have removed market risk from the equation.

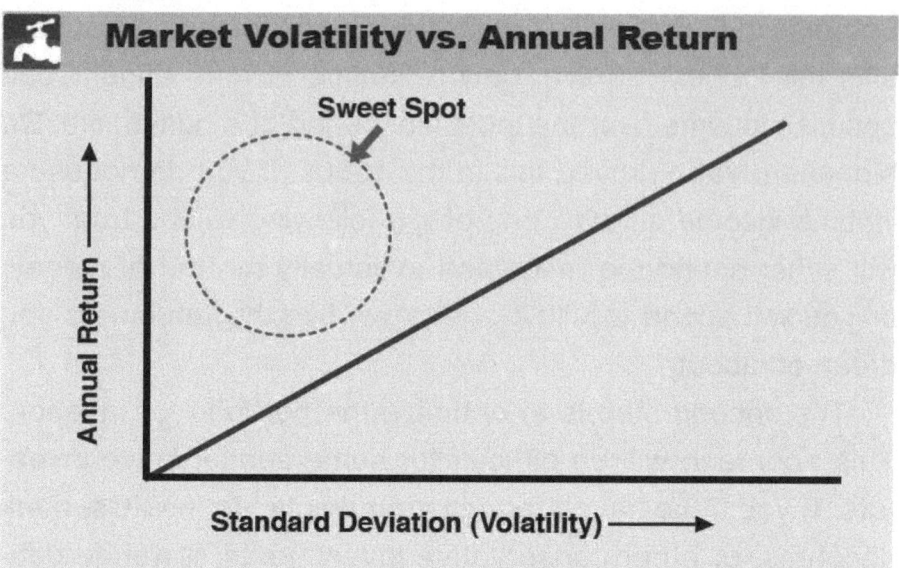

Market Volatility vs. Annual Return

Sweet Spot

Annual Return

Standard Deviation (Volatility) ⟶

Market volatility is measured by a mathematical concept called standard deviation. Generally, a higher standard deviation means greater volatility (and risk) but larger potential return. Our objective is to move your income-generating investments to the sweet spot of higher annual returns and less volatility.

What is the primary remaining risk? Inflation! So the optimization of the rest of your portfolio has to take inflation into account. Canada experienced high inflation during the 1970s, but then reverted to a long period of price stability. However, given recent international government policies, it is possible we could see higher inflation rates in the future. Even relatively low inflation rates will erode your purchasing power over time and you will become steadily poorer if you do not plan for it. Investments such as cash, savings accounts, or GICs that return less than the inflation rate will not protect you from inflation risk. CDIC insurance will not protect you from inflation risk. Having comfort in how liquid your money is in a money market fund will not protect you from inflation risk. Knowing you have some cash in a safety deposit box will not protect you from inflation risk.

Consider some alternative investments, such as putting some gold in your safe deposit box. Get some additional income from oil, gas, or other commodities. Invest in some of the greatest Canadian or global companies—RBC, TD, CIBC, Tim Horton's, Apple, Microsoft, Exxon, Google, Walmart, McDonald's, just to name a few. These are the ways to help protect your assets against inflation. Since your basic expenses are covered through guaranteed income (CPP/OAS, pension, and lifetime income annuities), you can afford to put part of your portfolio in more volatile investments as a hedge against inflation.

The Other Big Threats: Death and Disability

What are some of the other risks in retirement that we discussed? An early death may not be a problem for you (since you are dead). However, it may be a huge financial problem for your spouse, your parents, or your children. Earlier, we asked you to imagine your death. Who would be affected and how? What did you want to have happen, which now will not happen? We discussed the importance of life insurance—that it is actually a miracle product that produces exactly the right amount of money at exactly the right time.

We looked at all of the types of life insurance—term, whole life, universal life. The bottom line? The only policy that matters is the one that is in force when you die! Since death is a permanent problem, it is best solved with permanent life insurance.

A serious illness is another risk to both you and your family. Do you have critical illness insurance? Do you have a plan for long-term care (yes, you do, but is it a good plan)? Will you have to spend down your hard-earned money on a nursing home or rely only on limited government assistance? Will you be able to stay in your house instead of going into a nursing home? If you arrange your plan right, you will be able to stay in your home as long as you want without losing your life's savings—complete with your own nurse! If you want to move into assisted living—it will be your choice! No retirement plan is complete without a plan for long-term care!

The Ratings Game

Say you follow all of our advice. Are there other risks to retirement? The remaining risk is one that we have talked around but never specifically talked about—the credit risk of the insurance company itself. Many of the strategies we've discussed involve insurance companies, and not all insurance companies are created equal. Ratings matter—they matter more today than ever! How can we say that after the rating companies let us all down in the 2008 market implosion?

We can tell you that you have to remain very vigilant about the financial strength of whatever company or companies you use. Each year, read their annual report. Read the rating agencies' commentaries about them. The rating agencies are not perfect, but they do a tremendous amount of research and digging. The agencies are now subject to new rules and regulations regarding transparency and conflicts of interest. They will uncover significant risks and will write about them. Stick to the highest-rated companies and you will be served well. It is not worth reaching down the credit spectrum for an extra 20 bucks a month.

Get Real: Real Problems, Real Solutions

We have shared some simple ways real people have solved real problems. Those who will convert their RRSPs to a RRIF now know how to maximize the required minimum withdrawal to allow themselves to live a fantastic retirement—the retirement they always said they were going to have. We shared our belief that you do not owe your kids a penny of your retirement savings. Leave them the house, the cars, life insurance, and any other left over money, but do not lower your lifestyle in retirement for them!

We talked about registered plans and a recovery plan after a bear market. We responded to the usual objections to using lifetime income annuities—giving up control and liquidity, locking in low interest rates, that there are "better" ways to do this. Liquidity is not a one-time event—it is a lifetime event. A lifetime income annuity increases lifetime liquidity. By giving up control of a small portion of your savings, you gain control over many of the risks that you would not be able to control otherwise. We showed you how interest rates are responsible for only a small portion of the lifetime income annuity paycheque—especially at older ages. We showed you how to use laddering so that you are not putting your money into just one lifetime income annuity, but rather buying multiple annuities over time. As far as a "better" way of doing it, we would challenge any financial advisor to show us a better way that he or she can support with hard data.

123 Reverse Mortgage for Additional Liquidity – Buyer Beware

If you own a home and the property is your primary residence, you may qualify for a reverse mortgage. Basically, a reverse mortgage allows you to turn your home equity into cash in the form of monthly payments. In the event that you need some liquidity, a reverse mortgage could be useful. However, they can be expensive, with high closing costs, and the terms can be complicated and confusing. It is important to get independent advice from a qualified lawyer and financial advisor before entering into one of these arrangements.

Open-Minded Investors vs. Closed-Minded Advisors

We believe a few financial advisors may criticize this book as too heavily slanted towards insurance and insurance-based products like annuities. Why didn't we spend equal time discussing no-load mutual funds, managed money, ETFs (Exchange Traded Funds), options, futures, currencies, and whatever other investments are out there? Here is our answer: We support the use of all of these other products when appropriate.

We have used options in cases where we want to use some leverage on investments that we believe will appreciate. The real danger with options is that you not only have to be right—you have to be right at the right time. We have used mutual funds—both load and no-load. We like mutual funds for the simple reason that we believe the professionals can probably invest better than we can—even though we stay very connected to the markets. There are some great money managers out there and you should take advantage of the most talented ones. We also used ETFs in our investing strategies. ETFs are really just mutual funds that you can trade in real time—just like a stock or bond. Normal mutual funds have a daily settlement. You can buy or sell at the closing price. With an ETF, you can buy and sell throughout the day. As far as futures and currencies, these are generally not do-it-yourself projects. You can lose money very quickly if you do not know what you are doing.

The reason this book did not focus on those investments is because we do not think most retirees want the risk and volatility associated with many of these investments. They certainly are not appropriate to cover basic expenses. Basic expenses need to be covered by guaranteed income. If a product is used that does not contain mortality credits, the math and science will show that it is sub-optimal. Some people will say they can do better than a lifetime income annuity. The truth is that some will do better. However, many will do worse—and many of those will run out of money.

There are advisors out there recommending plans that have a 70% chance of success. If you were flying across the country and the airline told you they have a 70% chance of making it, only a 30% chance that they would crash—would you get on that plane? No way! Yet should you trust your retirement plan to an advisor who says you have a 70, 80, or even 90% chance of success? With a 90% likelihood of success, it still means that at least one out of 10 goes broke. If that person were you, you would not care that the other 90% were okay. The truth is that if you ran out of money, many of the other 90% would likely be in trouble as well.

All of these other investments may certainly have a place in the inflation planning part of portfolio optimization. In fact, by covering basic expenses with guaranteed income, the rest of the portfolio is much more likely to succeed. You can actually justify taking more risk with it. If you want to learn more about those types of investments, check out some of the experts who have written books about them. The important thing is to keep an open mind, ask good questions, and use common sense when discussing and evaluating investment options.

Closing Thoughts...

We wrapped up the book with a look at estate planning. We looked at wills, trusts, gifting, and life insurance. The chapter was not intended to be a detailed look at all of the latest estate planning techniques. Again, there are experts in this area who write books and articles. Estate planning is not a do-it-yourself project either. You need to take advantage of the financial advisors and lawyers who specialize in this area. Estate planning is all about minimizing taxes to you and your family and maximizing your assets to do exactly what you would like them to do after you are gone.

We said at the beginning of the book that we weren't going to give you opinions—we were going to stick to math and science. We would encourage you to read the writings of Dr. Moshe Milevsky, Dr. David Babbel, and Dr. Menahem Yaari. These gentlemen are truly experts in the area of retirement income. You can find their works in many places on the Internet.

In summary, retirement is not about assets! Assets can be lost, stolen, swindled, sued, divorced or decimated by a market crash. No, retirement is all about INCOME—and we would say Guaranteed Lifetime Income! It is also about reducing risks in retirement. So the optimal retirement would really follow these 4 simple steps:

> 1. Cover your basic expenses with Guaranteed Lifetime Income—this reduces longevity risk (since it is a guaranteed paycheque for life), it reduces deflation risk (since you are getting a paycheque, if prices actually go down during a

recession or depression, you are protected), it reduces market risk, withdrawal rate risk, and order of returns risk. See, you really take 5 key risks off the table when you cover your basic expenses with Guaranteed Lifetime Income.

2. Optimize the rest of your portfolio to protect yourself from inflation. Long term, you must protect yourself from the ravages of inflation. Stocks, Real Estate and some commodities have historically done a good job with inflation protection.

3. You MUST have a plan for Long-Term Care. No retirement plan is complete without a plan for Long-Term Care. It is the ONE thing most people forget about that can literally wipe out their portfolio.

4. The most efficient way to transfer wealth upon your death is to use permanent Life Insurance. Too many people use money to leave money. They have $200,000 in some "just in case account" that is meant to go to the kids. They could have taken $50,000 to buy a $200,000 policy for the kids and then used the other $150,000 for their OWN retirement. See, it is all about using your resources the most efficient way possible!

What we do know is this: if you follow the basic blueprint we have shared with you in this book, whether we have inflation, deflation, hyperinflation, or another Great Depression, you will live a happy and successful retirement. You will not have the stress and frustrations of your neighbors. Just educate yourself on the basics and seek qualified advice when needed. You worked so hard for this time in your life. These are now the best years of your life—go and live them to their fullest!

Appendix: The Math and Science of Retirement Income

If you have ever heard Tom speak, you have no doubt heard him talk about the "math and science" of a proper retirement. The person he quotes most often in his talks is Dr. Menahem Yaari. If you do some research on Dr. Yaari, you will find he had really set the economic world on fire with his analysis of consumer behavior and lifetime income annuities. In a 1965 article, he put forth the theory that a retiree who wanted to maximize his income would put all of his money into a lifetime income annuity. According to Dr. Yaari, there was no alternative that could guarantee a more "optimal" solution. The reason has everything to do with mortality credits. The risk pool can pay more than a person trying to maximize income on their own. Now, we are not recommending full annuitization. Dr. Yaari assumed that the retiree would not consider passing on money to heirs.

The benefits of an annuity-heavy portfolio are reiterated, 40 years later, in a study called "Annuities and Individual Welfare." While the authors give possible reasons for not fully annuitizing a portfolio, they prove that in most cases, significant investments in annuities were optimal. The low utilization rate of annuities by U.S. retirees was not rational and was "plausibly due to psychological or behavioral biases."

A Shift in Time

One of the modern day heroes of retirement income is a gentleman by the name of Moshe A. Milevsky. He has written many pieces on the importance of using annuities in retirement. In one of his articles, he said that the way most people have taken money in retirement historically was by using a well-diversified portfolio of stocks, bonds, real estate, and the normal investment classes, then withdrawing a fixed amount from principal, dividends, and interest. However, this "do it yourself" strategy will likely fail if you live too long or continue to withdraw money during an extended bear market.

Milevsky went on to state in this paper, as many revered analysts have before and since, that very few people actually annuitize their wealth even though countless studies have shown that this is exactly what they should do. Where Milevsky's study really differs from the others is in its attempt to determine when and how much a person should invest in annuities. For those over age 70 or 75, the evidence is really overwhelming on the side of annuities. However, for those younger than age 70, Milevsky makes a case for delaying annuitization, that the internal "load" or cost of the contract may not outweigh the benefits of the mortality credits. We will say that this paper was written prior to the lost decade of the stock market from 2000-2010 and the increased volatility of recent years.

Milevsky also wrote a paper with Virginia R. Young, which built on Milevsky's earlier paper and made some amendments. First, it highlighted that the more risk-tolerant someone is, the more they may want to delay shifting to annuities. Conversely, the more conservative an investor is, the earlier they would want to annuitize. We will say, again, that this paper was written prior to all of this market volatility we have experienced in recent years.

The Emerging Consensus

George Bernard Shaw once said, "If you laid all the economists end to end, they still wouldn't reach a conclusion." David Babbel, a Professor of the Insurance and Risk Management Department and Finance Department at the University of Pennsylvania, proved that Shaw's time-honored quote no longer holds true when it comes to using annuities for a "substantial portion of retirement wealth." Economists from coast to coast now agree that annuities are the best way to go. The list of the economists who have discovered this, includes some of the most prominent in the world, among whom are Nobel Prize winners. David Babbel and Craig Merrill wrote in a 2007 piece, "The tremendous value that annuities provide in retirement seems to be an area where most economists agree."

Babbel and Merrill go on to say that you should start by covering 100% of your minimum acceptable level of retirement income with annuities. This approach provides the most cost-effective and practical way to provide for security in retirement. Even after covering these basic expenses, you will still need to put a significant amount of your remaining portfolio in annuities while still investing some in stocks, bonds, and money market funds. We would add to this slightly, because we believe extra attention needs to be paid in the optimization phase to inflation-protected investments like gold, silver, oil, and real estate. Like Milevsky, Babbel says that while they can certainly complement the portfolio, stocks and bonds are no substitutes for annuities.

A Small Price to Pay

For those of you who believe that annuities cost too much, Professors Babbel and Merrill have some food for thought. The market for annuities has become so competitive that the fees (called "loadings") are extremely low. When you compare the one-time 0%-5% internal "loading" with the 1%-2% annual fees charged by mutual funds and managed money or back-end charges, which can be as high as 6%, the lifetime income annuities compare very well. They also remind readers that lifetime income annuities offer guaranteed income for life—something that mutual funds or managed money cannot do.

When asked if it would not be cheaper to cut out the insurer and create a "homemade" strategy, Babbel and Merrill reply that it would be great if something like that existed, but it is a fantasy. They could not find people saying the same thing about life insurance. And why not? Because it takes an insurance company to group a large enough risk pool of literally thousands of people all paying premiums. These premiums fund the death benefits that go to the people who die prematurely. The exact concept, in reverse, is what insurance companies do with lifetime income annuities.

As far as giving up control of some of the funds, Babbel and Merrill argue that far from being a disadvantage, giving up some control for guaranteed income is actually a smart move. Many people get frail as they age; their judgment becomes impaired. Think of how many older people have been taken advantage of not only by strangers, but by their own families. They become vulnerable to pressure to help their children and others with their retirement funds. Many people have lost everything in cases like this. Annuities also reduce the risk that people will withdraw too much or overspend. Babbel and Merrill conclude: "Sometimes we pay a very high price for maintaining what we think is control."

In 2010, Scott DeMonte and Lawrence Petrone, CFA of the Financial Research Corporation of Boston (FRC), produced a white paper for New York Life. The title of the document is "Income Annuities Improve Portfolio Outcomes in Retirement." Here is a cogent quote from their white paper:

> "Income Annuities offer features others can't—high cash flow, uncorrelated to market returns; retirement alpha in the form of mortality credits, which only life insurance companies can manufacture; longevity hedging and liquidity features."

That sounds to us like exactly what someone would be looking for in a retirement income vehicle.

A Class by Themselves

As far as optimizing retirement income and retirement security, DeMonte and Petrone emphasized that their analysis found that there was no other investment vehicle—none—that could match the income annuity for providing retirement security. No other investment vehicle was as efficient in creating retirement income from assets. They went on to say that no other investment could generate more income per dollar of capital than the income annuity, and that they "perfectly hedge longevity risk." Now, think about what they are saying—there is no other vehicle—none—in the market today that rivals the income annuity for providing income and peace of mind in retirement!

Many financial planners and brokers use age 90 as the maximum age for retirement income plan illustrations. We believe they do this because their plans will not hold up much beyond that. Even though most people do not think they will live to age 90, the facts are very different. Keep in mind that 33% of men, 44% of women, and 63% of married couples will have at least one of them live beyond age 90. Therefore, if you are married and you set up a financial plan that will last until age 90, that plan will fail 63% of the time.

DeMonte and Petrone also looked at using other sources of income instead of income annuities. Their focus was on successful outcomes. They found that because of the mortality credits paid from a lifetime income annuity and the guarantee of lifetime cheques, longevity risk is taken off the table. This more often than not ensures a successful outcome using a lifetime income annuity.

Don't Retire Without One

Few financial advisors have made the transition from accumulation to distribution. They still use systematic withdrawals from diversified portfolios or bond ladders to provide income. These investment vehicles subject their clients to market risk, interest rate risk, withdrawal risk, order of return risk, and, most significantly, longevity risk. To those advisors, the FRC report says: "We have proven that even a well-constructed moderate portfolio is likely to fail over the long term if investors get aggressive with withdrawal rates as many will." What is aggressive? Today, a 4% or more withdrawal rate is considered to be aggressive.

DeMonte and Petrone go on to say that financial advisors have the obligation of ensuring that their clients have successful financial outcomes no matter the economic storms we face. High inflation, market downturns, and medical advances in longevity are all examples of these storms. Our question is a simple one: if a financial advisor does not use a lifetime income annuity, then optimizes the rest of the portfolio with an eye on inflation, how can he do that? The answer is: he can't.

The FRC report adds that most investors do not understand the secret sauce of income annuities—namely the mortality credits (think of it as a new form of alpha or investment return).

Only life insurance companies can manufacture mortality credits. It is these mortality credits that allow a lifetime income annuity to have such high guaranteed payouts. No other investment can do this. That simply means that you cannot use futures, options, hedge funds, or any other vehicle to do what the lifetime income annuities can do!

Here is something interesting: did you know that the life insurance industry has a limited amount of mortality credits and therefore has a limited number of lifetime income annuities it can sell? This was news to us! We did not realize that the supply of income annuities is limited. Therefore, in 10 or 15 years, these products may be priced very differently than they are today.

As a demonstration of the significant income possibilities using a lifetime income annuity, the FRC report said, "Currently, income payout rates from AAA insurers for a 75-year-old male are at 8.9%, a 770 bps spread over the 1.2% 5-year Treasury." DeMonte and Petrone also noted that this product is perfect for the baby boomers who will be retiring in record numbers. They are coming into retirement with damaged portfolios. The credit crisis, dot-com dot-bomb, housing bubble, and euro crisis have really done a number on them. They will be seeking guarantees and less risk, and will be drawn to the high guaranteed income offered by lifetime income annuities.

For people who tend to shop for the highest payout rate, the FRC report cautions that ratings for lifetime income annuities are even more important than ratings on bonds since you are tied to a life insurance company for the rest of your life. It would be a big mistake to go with a lower-rated insurance company to try to squeeze out an extra $15 a month. The financial strength of the insurance company should be paramount in the buying decision. As Babbel has noted in his studies, the financial strength of the insurer is very important. The website SeekingAlpha.com puts it this way: "There are no more guarantees, only guarantors."

The FRC report found the following about adding a lifetime income annuity to a diversified portfolio: The portfolios that did not contain an income annuity significantly underperformed the portfolios that had a lifetime income annuity. Look, there is a simple test that you can do to try to prove all of this research wrong. Take any diversified portfolio (it must have both stocks and bonds), remove some of the bonds, and replace them with a lifetime income annuity. You know what it will do to that portfolio? It will reduce the risk to the portfolio and increase the returns! Here is why: when you add a lifetime income annuity to a portfolio, it functions like an AAA bond (with a CCC yield and zero standard deviation or volatility). Try it. See if you can prove us wrong.

We do not want this to be a technical, geeky book. But we have to provide enough evidence for you to feel comfortable with our recommendations. For those who want to do more research, there are websites you can go to for more technical information.

What Does The Media Say About Lifetime Income Annuities?

- "...a person would have been consistently better off buying an annuity at retirement, even at earlier ages... compared [to] the income paid out by annuities with a RRIF invested 50% in equities... the annuity won."

"The reason the annuity compares so well is because the insurance companies know that some annuitants will die young. They build the survivorship data into their annuity pricing which means if you are one of the lucky ones who live longer than average, you will do better with an annuity than with a RRIF."

Fred Vettesse

"Surprise! Annuities Beat RRIFs" *Financial Post*

(May 11, 2013)

- "Insurance companies carry a number of products - such as annuities and guaranteed minimum withdrawal benefit plans—that can provide you with guaranteed income for life."

Paul Russell

"Retirement: 10 Things You Need to Know" *The Star*

(August 3, 2010)

- "Retirement satisfaction has steadily declined over the last decade…"

"Satisfaction is highest among those with high levels of wealth and income who are very healthy and annuitize their income."

"Among retirees with similar wealth and health characteristics, those with annuitized incomes are happiest."

"Annuities provide the biggest satisfaction boost to retirees with less wealth and those in poor health"

Steve Nyce and Billie Jean Quade

"Annuities and Retirement Happiness"

Towers Watson White Paper

September 2012

- "Economists have long argued that there's a perfect financial product for retirement: the humble immediate income annuity...Proponents argue that income annuities protect not only against longevity risk, but the risk of under-spending in retirement."

Mark Miller
"The Income Annuity Puzzle:
Why don't more people use them?" *Rueters*
(Aug 19, 2013)

- "Many Investors approaching retirement think they have no need for annuities. But the lifetime-income guarantees offered by these insurance-company products can add security to portfolios that are mostly composed of stock and bond mutual funds."

Lavonne Kuykendall
"Making the Case to Buy an Annuity"
The Wall Street Journal
(March 8, 2011)

• "The happiest people in retirement were those who had a stream of guaranteed paychecks for life. Some had pensions. The others purchased lifetime income annuities."

Jonathon Clements
"The Secret to Happier Retirement" in WSJ.com
(July 5, 2005)

Jonathan Clements looked at what the happiest people in retirement had in common. He listed seven common traits, including surrounding yourself with friends and neighbors, who you get along with, thinking ahead, and getting a guaranteed stream of income.

SOURCES BY CHAPTER

PREFACE

Mark Whitehouse, "Fed's Low Interest Rates Crack Retiree's Nest Eggs," *Wall Street Journal*, April 4, 2011, http://online.wsj.com/article/SB100014240527487034106045762168309 41163492.html

CHAPTER 1

"S&P 500 pensions, OPEBS remain underfunded," *BenefitsPro*, May 26, 2011, http://www. benefitspro.com/2011/05/26/sp-500-pensions-opebs-remain-underfunded

"The Underfunding of State and Local Pension Plans," Congressional Budget Office, May 2011, http://www.cbo.gov/ftpdocs/120xx/doc12084/05-04-Pensions.pdf

"Life Expectancy at Birth, Total (years)." *The World Bank*. World Back, 2014. April 14, 2014,http://data.worldbank.org/indicator/SP.DYN.LE00.IN/countries/CA--XS?display=graph

"Weekly Spot Price - West Texas Intermediate Crude," U.S. Energy Information Agency, http://www.eia.gov/dnav/pet/hist/LeafHandler.ashx?n=pet&s=rwtc&f=w

Marcy Nicholson and Mihir Dalal, "Smucker hikes Folgers coffee 11 pct in fourth rise," *Reuters*, May 24, 2011, http://www.reuters.com/article/2011/05/24/jmsmucker-idU-SL3E- 7GO1RJ20110524

"Annual Report of the Canada Pension Plan 2012-2013." *Employment and Social Development Canada*. Government of Canada, April 14, 2014, http://www.esdc.gc.ca/eng/retirement/reports/annual_cpp2013.shtml

Stephanie Clifford and Catherine Rampell, "Food Inflation Kept Hidden in Tinier Bags," *New York Times*, March 28, 2011, http://www.nytimes.com/2011/03/29/business/29shrink.html?_r=11

"Medicare rates could eat up raise in Social Security," *Associated Press*, March 28, 2011,http://www.toledoblade.com/local/2011/03/28/Medicare-rates-could-eat-up-raise-in-Social-Security.html

Mark Sarney, "Distributional Effects of Price Indexing Social Security Benefits," U.S. Social Security Administrations, November 2010, http://www.ssa.gov/policy/docs/policybriefs/ pb2010-03.html

"2011 Annual Report of the Board of Trustees of the Federal Hospital Insurance Trust Fund and the Federal Supplementary Medical Insurance Trust Fund," Boards of Trustees for Medicare, May 13, 2011, https://cms.gov/reportstrustfunds/downloads/tr2011.pdf

Stanley Pignal, "Brussels to Press for Higher Retirement Ages," *Financial Times*, July 4, 2010, http://www.ft.com/cms/s/0/fe168510-87b0-11df-9f37-00144feabdc0.html

Richard Jackson, "China's Long March to Retirement Reform," *ChinaStakes*, October 26, 2009, http://www.chinastakes.com/2009/5/chinas-long-march-to-retirement-reform.html

Karen Hube, "Special Report - Retirement: With their steady income payments, annuities are suddenly hot, *Barron's*, June 20, 2011, http://online.barrons.com/article/SB50001424053111904472004576392401608661120.html

"Retirement Income - Ensuring Income Throughout Retirement Requires Difficult Choices," GAO Report to the Chairman, Special Committee on Aging, U.S. Senate, June 2011, http:// www.gao.gov/new.items/d11400.pdf

CHAPTER 2

EllenSchultz, "Rosy Assumptions Could Wreck Your Retirement," *Wall Street Journal*, June 18, 2011, http://onlinewsj.com/article/SB100014240527023044533045763 9173423131810 2.html

Suzanne Barlyn, "Live Very Very Long and Prosper," *Wall Street Journal,* June 27, 2011, http://finance.yahoo.com/focus-retirement/article/112977/live-very-very-long-and- prosper=wsj?mod=fidelity-buildingwealth&cat=fidelity_2010_building_wealth

Ralph Silberman, "Survey: MetLife Reports that Pre-Retirees Overestimate Retirement Moneys and Underestimate Retirement Length and Needs," *Aging Workforce News*, June 27, 208, http://www.agingworkforcenews.com/2008_06_01_archive.html

Jonathon Clemens, "How to Survive Retirement - Even if You're Short on Savings," *Wall Street Journal,* January 17, 2007, http://online.wsj.com/article/SB116899974081778389. html

Laura Shrestha, "Life Expectancy in the United States," Report for Congressional Research Service, August 16, 2006, http://aging.senate.gov/crs/aging1.pdf

Scott DeMonte and Lawrence Petrone, "Income Annuities Improve Portfolio Outcomes in Retirement," Financial Research Corporation report, 2010

John Mauldin, "Inflation and Deflation: Navigating the Curve in the Road," *Seeking Alpha,* April 11, 2011 (see comments), http://seekingalpha.com/article/262789-inflation-and-deflation-navigating-the-curve-in-the-road

Joe Morgan, "Buy tear gas stocks, Greece Police running out of gas pellets¼," *Seeking Alpha*, posted on June 29, 2011, http://seekingalpha.com/user/764315/stocktalk/1839136

CHAPTER 3

Suzanne Barlyn, "Live Very Very Long and Prosper," *Wall Street Journal*, June 27, 2011, http://finance.yahoo.com/focus-retirement/article/112977/live-very-very-long-and- prosper=wsj?mod=fidelity-buildingwealth&cat=fidelity_2010_building_wealth

CHAPTER 4

Alain Theriault, Segregated Funds: Net Sales Sink," *The Insurance & Investment Journal*, March 7, 2012, http://www.insurance-journal.ca/2012/03/07/segregated-funds-net-sales-sink/

"TD Science & Technology GIF," *TD Asset Management*, April 15, 2014, https://www.tdas-setmanagement.com/fundDetails.form?fundId=3567&prodGroupId=10&lang=en&site=AssetManagement#

"Insurance Act," ServiceOntario, 1990, https://www.e-laws.gov.on.ca/html/statutes/english/elaws_statutes_90i08_e.htm

CHAPTER 5

John Bledsoe, The Gospel of Roth: The Good News About Roth IRA Conversions and How They Can Make You Money, LandMarc Press Inc., Hardcover edition (January 12, 2010)

"RRSPs and Other Registered Plans for Retirement," *Canada Revenue Agency*, 2014, http:// www.cra-arc.gc.ca/E/pub/tg/t4040/t4040-e.html

"Canada Pension Plan payment amounts," *Service Canada*, 2014, http://www.servicecanada.gc.ca/eng/services/pensions/cpp/payments/

CHAPTER 6

Bob Graham, "Variable annuity sales better than overall annuity numbers in 2010," *Insurance & Financial Advisor News*, Feburary 16, 2011, http://ifawebnews.com/2011/02/16/variable-annuity-sales-better-than-overall-annuity-numbers-in-2010/

John Huggard, JD, CFP, Investing with Variable Annuities: Fifty Reasons Why Variables Annuities May Be Better Long-Term Investments Than Mutual Funds, Parker-Thompson Publishing, 1st edition (June 1, 2002)

E.S. Browning, "Exercising Ghosts of Octobers Past," *Wall Street Journal*, October 15, 2007, http://onlinewsj.com/article/SB119239926667758592.html

"Manulife Investments enhances Canada's first Guaranteed Minimum Withdrawal Benefit product," *Manulife Financial*, September 22, 2008, https://www.manulife.com/public/news/detail/0,,lang=en&artId=143746&navId=630002,00.html

Carolyn T. Geer, "The great annuity rip-off," *Forbes*, February 9, 1998, http://www.forbes.com/forbes/1998/0209/6103106a.html

CHAPTER 7

Emily Flynn Vencat, "Narcissists in Neverland," *Newsweek*, October 15, 2007, http://www.thedailybeast.com/newsweek/2007/10/15/narcissists-in-neverland.html

Kimberly Lankford, "Life Insurance After 50," *Kiplinger's Personal Finance*, June 2011, http://www.kiplinger.com/magazine/archives/life-insurance-after-50.html

CHAPTER 8

The 2010 Sourcebook for Long-Term Care Insurance, American Association For Long-Term Care Insurance, data by Milliman Consulting (2010)

Medicare & You Handbook, Centers for Medicare & Medicaid Services (2011), http://www.medicare.gov/publications/pubs/pdf/10050.pdf

"CLHIA Report on Long-Term Care Policy," *Canadian Life and Health Insurance Association*, June 2012, http://www.clhia.ca/domino/html/clhia/CLHIA_LP4W_LND_Webstation.nsf/resources/Content_PDFs/$file/LTC_Policy_Paper.pdf

"Your Million Dollar Problem," *Guide to Long-Term Care website*, 2011, http://www.guideto-longtermcare.com/milliondollarproblem.html

CHAPTER 9

Laura Saunders, "The State of the Estate Tax," *Wall Street Journal*, December 11, 2010, http://online.wsj.com/article/SB100014240527487047208045760099627526888894.html

Linda Koco, "Is Estate Planning Dead?" *InsuranceNewsNet Magazine*, February 2011

CHAPTER 10

Peter Tchir, "Sovereign Debt: Has Europe Finally Discovered Alchemy?" *Seeking Alpha*, July 21, 2011, http://seekingalpha.com/article/280939-sovereign-debt-has-europe-finally-discovered-alchemy

APPENDIX

Menahem Yaari. "Uncertain Lifetime, Life Insurance, and the Theory of the Consumer." *Review of Economic Studies*. 32.2 (1965): 137-50.

T. Davidoff, J.R. Brown, & P.A. Diamond. "Annuities and Individual Welfare." *American Economic Review*. 95.5 (2005): 1573-90.

Moshe A. Milevsky. "Optimal Asset Allocation Towards the End of the Life Cycle: To Annuitize or Not to Annuitize?" *The Journal of Risk and Insurance*. 65.3 (1998): 401-26.

M.A. Milevsky & V.R. Young. "Optimal Asset Allocation and the Real Option to Delay Annuitization: It's Not Now-or-Never." *Working Paper*, York University (2002).

D. Babbel & C. Merrill. "Investing Your Lump Sum at Retirement." The Wharton School, University of Pennsylvania (2007).

Acknowledgments

This book has been 25 years in the making. Because of that, I have many people to thank. There are some groups of people who have had a lasting impact on me and on what I do. I believe there are only a few times in your entire life where you get to work with a superior team. Times when you really have fun going to work every day; times when you are surrounded by talented people and you all work better together than apart. I have been fortunate to experience that several times in my life.

When Rob and Steve reached out to me I knew we needed to take these ideas to Canada. Rob and Steve are experts in their field and they exposed me to a lot of pertinent information for Canadian residents. Regardless of where you are in the world, you need to have a plan for your retirement. Without their expert advice, I wouldn't have been able to complete the book.

Raised in a small town in Minnesota, I grew up with an interest in money. Maybe it was because we didn't have much—I'm really not sure. I would collect coins and spend hours sorting through them looking to fill the holes in my coin collection books. I would exchange these coins at the bank almost daily. As a young boy, I sold seeds door to door to earn spending money. Perhaps some of my very best business education came when I worked as a paperboy. I had two routes and delivered newspapers every day for years. Today, I cannot imagine allowing my 10 or 11-year-old children to go out by themselves every morning, in the dark, in -25 degree weather. But that is what I did— every day—rain or shine. I actually enjoyed delivering papers in the crisp, Minnesota air. The hard part of a paper route was that you also had to collect the money from the subscribers. So every two weeks, I had to go door to door again (this time in the evening) alone, to collect the money. It was amazing to hear all of the excuses people made as to why they couldn't pay the $2.50 they owed for the two weeks! I really learned a lot about people and selling in those formative years. I also learned that hard work pays off: I always had a new bicycle, the best hockey equipment, and almost anything else that I really wanted. I earned trips to see the Harlem Globetrotters, Minnesota Twins and Minnesota North Stars. I learned early that hard work and self-discipline yield incredible results—regardless of your age or station in life. I also learned how important giving to others is. I am a firm believer in giving 10% or more each year to help others that are less fortunate than I have been. At my core, I am still a military officer. I attended college on an Army ROTC scholarship, spent 6 years on Active Duty in the Army, and another 16½ years in the Army Reserve. I retired in 2006 as a Lieutenant Colonel. Whenever I undergo tough situations or stress, my military background will come to the forefront. The army taught me discipline, selfless service, and mission accomplishment— on time, in time, and right the first time. It taught me to appreciate the simple things in life, which we ought to bask in each precious day. War should always be a last resort—never a first resort.

My toughest years in the Army were when I was in the 3rd Infantry Division in West Germany. It was right in the middle of the Cold War, and we had alerts in the middle of the night almost weekly. The times in my life when I was the coldest, the hungriest, and the most exhausted were those I spent in Germany.

Later, as a company commander in the 7th Infantry Division (Light) at Ft. Ord, California, I had my most enjoyable times. I had a company that could literally do anything it was called upon to do, and do it well. I had a team of lieutenants who were just superb. We got along great; we had fun, but we also had the highest standards in the division. Morale was exceptional and I loved going to work every day. I honed my leadership skills in that assignment. I learned how to set the vision, delegate, and then hold subordinates accountable. I found that 100 people working together can literally move mountains. One of my lieutenants, Mark Cincotta, has stayed a lifelong friend. I tried to recruit him when I was a MetLife manager, but he went on to build his own very successful career in the financial services industry.

In the Army Reserves, I was selected to command a battalion. I was selected as a major and was soon promoted to lieutenant colonel. Again, we had fun accomplishing each mission. Soldiers love to do their jobs well and be recognized for their achievements. I pinned many medals on my soldiers over the years. I would not be where I am without the great soldiers of the U.S. Army. Even in my civilian jobs, I am always kidded for my strict adherence to SOPs (Standard Operation Procedures, which are really the military's version of "best practices"). There are way too many to mention, but special shout-outs to General Perrin, COL Foster, COL Raynor, CW5 Raynor, CW4 Wad-dell, and LTC Barth.

When people ask me where I learned to speak as effectively as I do, I point to my military training. When you have to brief a general, you'd better have a full command of the subject you are briefing them on, or they will literally rip you to shreds right there in front of everyone. I have watched it happen to others many times. Before one of my briefings, I always ensured that I was well prepared—I knew the subject cold, I anticipated the questions, I even had a plan of how to answer something I didn't know. I also tried to have other subject matter experts present so I could introduce them to the general and solicit their knowledge on the subject as well.

Everyone has two or three people in their lives that have made all the difference in launching them to another level. Jack and Garry Kinder made a huge impact on my life. When I was hired to be an agent for MetLife, I just didn't feel the training was enough for me. However, there were some dusty VHS tapes in closet. The tapes were of the famous "Kinder Brothers." I watched those tapes over and over and over. I can still answer some of the objections word for word. I would not be where I am today without the Kinder Brothers—period.

Joe Jordan and Ted Kilkuskie were officers of MetLife. However, they weren't like any other "home office" people I had ever met before. They made meetings come to life. I learned how important language and words are. They had fun and were exceptionally creative in explaining new concepts. They made learning fun—I have since called this type of training "edutainment." I never missed a chance to see them in action. When I started speaking, it was Joe who said "Remember, Hegna: the bigger the audience, the bigger the show!" Joe was (and is) a showman extraordinaire. I wouldn't be where I am today without him. I would also like to thank Dennis Barghaan and Gary Olivero for the many great memories while we were on the Variable Products team. A number of my fellow MetLife agents went on to enjoy great success of their own: Wayne Kandas became the number one agent at MetLife; Sue Ritchie has a great long-term care insurance practice; Eric Feller and Mike Mazzella Jr. are running an independent brokerage operation; Todd Miller has a successful practice in the East Valley.

In 1996, I was recruited by Bob Meredith to join New York Life. Sy Sternberg, the new CEO, had agreed to provide product experts to support the New York Life field force as part of his "I owe you" agreement with the field. When Sy took over, morale in the field was low. In just a couple of years, he turned the entire thing around to create what is arguably the finest field force in the entire insurance industry. Bob Rock ran the annuity department along with his deputy, John Meyer. They created a very powerful team of product wholesalers who energized the field and saw production numbers skyrocket. Bob Meredith put together his "Dream Team" which included me, John O'Gara (who now leads all of the product wholesalers for New York Life), Alise Miller (who leads the investment and retirement wholesalers), Matt Vahl, Ray Lynch (retired), John O'Brien, Joe Watson (retired), Steve Sullivan, Chuck Staley, and Jim Robinson. We continued to hire the best and the brightest in the industry but that team was, I believe, the most productive team in company history. Ted Mathas was Sy's hand-picked replacement. Ted took the lifetime income annuity product off the shelf, shook the dust off it, and put in the resources necessary to really make it come to life. He saw the value in mortality credits when few others even knew what mortality credits were. He hired Chris Blunt, who is the Executive Vice President in charge of retirement security. Michael Gordon and Debbie Moy also played huge roles in the success of the Lifetime Income Annuity product. I would like to say a special thank you to all of my friends at New York Life. I spent 15 incredible years with these great agents, managers, and officers.

My big break happened in 2008. Former Million Dollar Round Table (MDRT) President and New York Life agent, Walton Rogers, recommended me to MDRT to be one of the speakers at the Boomertirement Roadshows that were sponsored by PREP (a combination of many different insurance industry associations). We did roadshows in Dallas, Chicago, Washington, D.C., New York, and Los Angeles. These were held right during the market meltdown in 2008. It seemed as though everyone was scared to death. Many financial advisors didn't know what to say to their clients. It seemed like a terrible time for nearly everyone.

And yet, there I stood on the stage, saying that our industry was "built for markets just like these! Our products—life insurance and annuities—were built for markets like these." I gave a message that was loud and clear and very positive: that we had the answers for our clients, not Wall Street. FinancialPlanning.com said this: "When New York Life (Vice) President Tom Hegna took the stage, he delivered a loud, boisterous presentation that served as a full-throated endorsement of the insurance business. He left to a standing ovation from the energized audience—an almost surreal moment of optimism for an industry that has been battered and bruised by mounting capital shortages and a series of ratings downgrades." The top industry leaders attended those meetings.

Phil Harriman, a past President of MDRT, really took me under his wing and made sure that every industry leader at those meetings met me. He helped get me in front of the right people and I got an invitation to speak on the main platform of the Top of the Table Meeting in Kauai in 2009! What a huge honor. From there, it was to the main platform of the MDRT Annual meeting in Vancouver. Understand that two to three thousand people are reviewed for just 18 main platform slots. To get one of these slots you have to be good, but also a little lucky—and your timing must be just right! Terry Headley, the incoming National Association of Insurance and Financial Advisors (NAIFA) President, then called me and asked me to be the opening speaker at the 2010 NAIFA annual meeting. Others who really went above and beyond in helping me were Jeff Taggart and Tom Currey (both past presidents of NAIFA), Julian Good and Jennifer Borislow (past and present presidents of MDRT, respectively), and Jim Tyrpak, President of the Society of Financial Services Professionals.

In addition to a tremendous professional network, I have also been fortunate to have the unending support of my parents, Dave and Fran Hegna of Fergus Falls, MN, and my sisters, Mary and Becky. I am so thankful for over 30 years of marriage with my wife, Laurie, and for our three sons Ryan (a successful entrepreneur in Tempe, AZ), Sean (an engineer for Eaton Corp.), and JJ (my 14-year-old athlete who is basically the identical twin of Ryan, although they are separated by 15 years).

JJ had a brain tumor six years ago and underwent seven hours of brain surgery. Brett Favre, Franco Harris, Lydell Mitchell, and John Runyan all visited JJ in the hospital, because the Super Bowl was in Phoenix the week of his surgery. We are all thrilled at the incredible work of Dr. Daniel Lieberman—we got the whole JJ back!

Then there is my 12-year-old daughter Samantha - Sami is a dancer, an artist, and a voracious reader. (She was very excited about being mentioned in my book.)

As for helping me with the book, Paige Stover-Hague and George Kasparian of Acanthus Publishing and her entire staff were fantastic. Robert and Steve from Canada were great to work with on this project. Other members of the Acanthus editorial team also contributed significantly to the project: Robert Roussel, Madeline Rau, David Kennedy Luke Messecar, Andrew Padgett, Eliza Rosenberry, Theresa Yannetty, Matt Angelosanto, Stephanie Mann, Gabrielle Corrado, Rodeline Prince, James Molinaro, Andrea Weidknecht, and Lois Hager. Ian Nichols, Tazuko Sugajima, and Morgan Laliberte, also on the staff of Acanthus Publishing, contributed the cover design, internal layout, and graphs and charts. Carolyn Burgess gave me some great input on the long-term care chapter. I travelled the country with Carolyn over the years doing many joint meetings.

Rob and Steve would also like to thank the contributions and consultative work of Michael Peters of White Rock, BC. Michael was essential with checking our Canada regulatory facts.

So, as I said, this book was really 25 years in the making —to be honest, I guess more like 50 years in the making. My entire life's experience went into the pages of this book. I hope you take at least a few good ideas to better your own financial life! Be on the lookout for my next book, which will be coming soon…

Tom Hegna
Fountain Hills, AZ
March, 2014